Passing the Principal

TExES

Exam

2
EDITION

This updated edition of Passing the Principal TExES Exam *remains dedicated to my beloved husband of 40 years, Greg Wilmore; my children, Brandon Greggory Wilmore and Brooke Elaine Wilmore; our daughter Brittani Wilmore Rollen, her awesome husband, Ryan, and their brilliant and beautiful daughter, my darling granddaughter, Blair Elaine Rollen; my late parents Lee and Irene Watson Litchfield; and all my friends, colleagues, and students who love and pray for me when I least deserve it. Thank you for being the wind beneath my wings and for always encouraging me to get back up when I fall down. I love you all.*

And Jabez prayed to the God of Israel saying,
"Oh, God, please bless me indeed
And enlarge my territory.
May your hand be with me.
Keep me from evil and
Let me not cause pain."
And God honored his request.

I Chronicles 4:10

I can do all things through Christ who
strengthens me.

Philippians 4:13

Lee and Irene Litchfield

2
EDITION

Passing the Principal
TExES
Exam

Keys to Certification
& School Leadership

Elaine L. Wilmore

Foreword by
Diane Patrick
Ph.D., Texas State House of Representatives,
District 94, Arlington

CORWIN
A SAGE Company

CORWIN
A SAGE Company

FOR INFORMATION:

Corwin
A SAGE Company
2455 Teller Road
Thousand Oaks, California 91320
(800) 233-9936
www.corwin.com

SAGE Publications Ltd.
1 Oliver's Yard
55 City Road
London EC1Y 1SP
United Kingdom

SAGE Publications India Pvt. Ltd.
B 1/I 1 Mohan Cooperative Industrial Area
Mathura Road, New Delhi 110 044
India

SAGE Publications Asia-Pacific Pte. Ltd.
3 Church Street
#10-04 Samsung Hub
Singapore 049483

Printed in the United States of America

A catalog record of this book is available from the Library of Congress.

ISBN 971452286013

Acquisitions Editor: Arnis Brvikovs
Associate Editor: Desirée A. Bartlett
Editorial Assistant: Mayan White
Production Editor: Amy Schroller
Copy Editor: Michelle Ponce
Typesetter: C&M Digitals (P) Ltd.
Proofreader: Victoria Reed-Castro
Indexer: Naomi Linzer
Cover Designer: Anupama Krishnan
Permissions Editor: Jennifer Barron

This book is printed on acid-free paper.

SUSTAINABLE FORESTRY INITIATIVE
Certified Chain of Custody
Promoting Sustainable Forestry
www.sfiprogram.org
SFI-01268
SFI label applies to text stock

13 14 15 16 17 10 9 8 7 6 5 4 3 2 1

Contents

Foreword

Preparing qualified and certified principal leaders for the schools of Texas is imperative to our future. In this second edition of *Passing the Principal TExES Exam: Keys to Certification and School Leadership*, Dr. Elaine Wilmore teaches important additional test-taking strategies and methods of data analysis, as well as continues to provide the theoretical framework, to help students pass this difficult statewide principal certification assessment.

Her writing style merges theory and the ideal practice of school leadership in a way that is concise, comprehensive, and even inspiring. Dr. Wilmore's vast experience as an educator, from teacher to principal to university professor, gives her unique insight into the effective principalship that translates into practical leadership development.

Adhering to the principles of Dr. Wilmore's first highly acclaimed exam preparation textbook has resulted in success for thousands of students across Texas. If you truly want to become the "Ideal Principal," and to pass the Texas Examination of Educator Standards, this new edition meets the highest of expectations.

Diane Patrick, PhD, is the current Texas State Representative from District 94, Arlington. She serves on the House Higher Education and Appropriations Committee, and is a former university professor, School Board Trustee, and State Board of Education Member.

—11-5-12

Preface

Passing the Principal TExES Examination: Keys to Certification and School Leadership was written to help educators in Texas pass the principal Texas Examinations of Educator Standards (TExES). The original 2002 edition became an instant Corwin best seller and remains as such to this day. It is used by universities and alternative preparation programs, as well as individual students, across the state. This second edition continues to be based on domains and competencies provided through Texas law (19 Texas Administrative Code Chapter 241.15) and developed by the Texas State Board for Educator Certification (SBEC) and the success of the original edition. It is written based on the years of experience Wilmore has as a teacher, counselor, principal, professor, and school board member and providing popular, successful, and inspiring TExES preparation seminars at universities, regional service centers, and other training sites around the state. In addition, this updated version also includes updates to the TExES exam and additional test-taking strategies developed since the original printing.

The nature of the book is both broad and specific. Part I provides the global overview, tools, and format of the book. Part II provides the philosophy and theoretical framework for TExES success. It details the Texas domains, competencies, and leadership philosophy on which TExES is constructed. Each of Part II's 10 chapters details a specific competency in a down-to-earth, interesting manner using real-life stories for practical application while engaging the reader and connecting theory to practice. Each chapter has the details necessary for proactive school leadership and TExES success, and the book closes with an extensive list of additional resources to supplement each domain. Section III ties the philosophy of TExES to other important test-taking concepts and techniques such as how to read and analyze data, manage time while testing, and use specific strategies to discern correct answers. It includes information about how to create an individualized personal success plan, how to prepare for the TExES, and what to do in the weeks, days, and night before the test. The book concludes with a minitest of applicable decision sets so readers can practice their skills.

Passing the Principal TExES Examination: Keys to Certification and School Leadership is a valued asset for current administrators seeking to refine, refocus, and develop their learner-centered leadership skills as well as helping aspiring administrators pass the TExES examination. With a proven record of success, the book will not only provide a solid theoretical framework for school leadership, it will make learning fun and inspire greatness. Readers will enjoy the book, be ready to pass the TExES exam, and then to change the world—one school at a time.

Acknowledgments

God has blessed me with such a wonderful family and so many great friends. It is simply impossible to acknowledge all of them for everything they have brought to my life. My books come from my heart and my faith as a gift to others. Without my family, friends, and my faith, where would my heart be? What would it hold?

So, in the simplest of words, thank you. Thank you to my husband, Greg, to our children Brandon and Brooke Wilmore, Brittani and Ryan Rollen, and our beautiful and brilliant granddaughter Blair Elaine. Thank you to our unborn grandson who we will get to meet this February! Welcome to our world!! Thank you to my friends that always surround me with love and support. It would be absolutely impossible to name all of you, but here are a few: Barbara Webb, Keith, Amy, Phoebe, Aaron, and Christian Burkman, Brenda, Sarah, Ben, Matt, Sam, Zach, Ella, Jeff, T. N., Larry and Diane Wilmore, Sophie and Tony Sarda, Marlene and Bill Carter, Wanda and John Rollen, Billie Westbrook, Helen and Wes Nelson, Dr. Joe and Kathy Martin, JoNell and Larry Jones, Donna and Milton Walker, Dr. Bob and Becky Shaw, Dr. Linda and Ron Townzen, Dr. Wade, Renea, and Emily Smith, Dr. Jesse Jai McNeil, Jr., Dr. Mary Lynn Crow, Bob and Sallie Feavel, and my lifelong beloved childhood friends Melda Cole Ward and Kerry Van Doren Pedigo. And, last but certainly not least, I must also thank my gracious and diligent teaching assistant, Maryanne Piña, for helping me beyond measure.

Few are blessed with the quality and quantity of my family and friends.

Last, I must always thank my parents, the late Lee and Irene Litchfield, to whom I owe all that I am or ever will be. They taught me values, faith, a sense of humor, and to love and care for others. They also always supported my lifelong love of reading, libraries, and all things related to books. I miss you both so much. We will be together again someday too in Heaven.

Love always,
Elaine

" . . . saying, I am Alpha and Omega, the first and the last: and, what thou seest, write in a book, . . ."

Revelation 1:11

About the Author

 **Elaine L. Wilmore**, PhD, is a remote online professor at Texas A&M University at Commerce as well as the owner of Elaine L. Wilmore Leadership Initiatives. She formerly served as Professor, Chair of Educational Leadership, Counseling, and Foundations and Doctoral Director at the University of Texas of the Permian Basin. She has previously served at Dallas Baptist University as Assistant Vice President for Educational Networking and Program Director for the MEd and EdD degrees in Educational Leadership. She has formerly served as special assistant to the Dean for NCATE Accreditation, Chair and Associate Professor of Educational Leadership and Policy Studies at the University of Texas at Arlington, President of the National Council of Professors of Educational Administration, President of the Texas Council of Professors of Educational Administration, and president of the Board of Trustees of the Cleburne Independent School District where she served for nine years. She is the founding director of the Dallas Baptist University EdD in Educational Leadership and multiple programs at the University of Texas at Arlington (UTA) including all initial programs, Educational Leadership UTA, and the Scholars of Practice Program. While at UTA, she was also principal investigator for multiple grants for innovative field-based principal preparation programs. She has served as Director of University Program Development at UTA where she also developed and was the original Chair of the Faculty Governance Committee for the College of Education. Dr. Wilmore is professionally active and has served on many local, state, and national boards. These include having served on the Executive Committee of the National Council Professors of Educational Administration, the American Educational Research Association Executive Committee on the Teaching in Educational Administration SIG, the Texas Principals Leadership Initiative, the Texas Consortium of Colleges of Teacher Education, and has served as a program/folio reviewer for the Educational Leadership Constituent Council. She holds the unique distinction of being one of the few to have served as both a private and public school district Board of Trustees member.

Dr. Wilmore was a public school teacher, counselor, elementary, and middle school principal before she moved to higher education. In addition to her significant work in educational leadership, assessment, and program development, she enjoys reading, writing, walking, traveling, music, and spending time with those she loves. She is the wife of Greg Wilmore; the only child of her late beloved parents, Lee and Irene Litchfield; the mother of three wonderful children, Brandon Greggory Wilmore, Brooke Elaine Wilmore, and Brittani Leigh Wilmore Rollen; and a fabulous son-in-law, Ryan Rollen. Top highlights of her life are her first grandchild, Miss Blair Elaine Rollen and a grandson who is expected in February 2013. Elaine has four outstanding Pug dogs named Annabella Rose, Isabella Lace, Zoe Eloise, and Tug the Pug that she loves dearly. In her limited spare time she dreams of learning to play the violin, viola, and cello and also taking leisurely hot, peach bubble baths by candlelight in Italy.

SECTION I

Content

The Knowledge Base

Welcome!

In the state of Texas, as in many other states, there is a rigorous certification examination that potential administrators must pass before they are eligible for certification. In Texas this test is called the TExES (Texas Examinations of Educator Standards). There is tremendous pressure on future leaders to pass this test. Without it, they cannot become certified. There is also tremendous pressure on preparation programs for their students to do well. Potential test takers from both inside and outside the state are looking for tools to help them achieve their goal of certification and reaching the principalship. This book describes how to become the world's best principal through awesome leadership preparation.

Universities and alternative preparation programs are working hard to address both the knowledge and the philosophical bases on which TExES is framed. The test is built on a foundation of nine competencies within three domains, and its creators assume that test takers have received knowledge and research preparation through their educational providers. This book supplies needed supplemental resources for the knowledge base, but it is not intended to substitute for a master's degree. It focuses, however, on the philosophy necessary to think like a learner-centered principal. Many students find it difficult to make the transition from thinking like a teacher to thinking, reflecting, reacting, and responding like a principal. All of the knowledge in the world is useless if a test taker cannot think in the way the test was developed. *Passing the Principal TExES Examination: Keys to Certification and School Leadership* addresses the philosophy as well as the skills that principals must have within each of the three domains and nine competencies. It provides test-taking tips for before, during, and after the exam. Specific attention is given to in-state and out-of-state test takers. The volume also provides practice test questions grouped into decision sets within a minitest. Each competency chapter concludes with additional resources that are helpful to students as they develop the knowledge and philosophical bases necessary to pass the test and pursue careers as lifelong learners.

Finally, this book is written in an informal, first-person voice. There are real-life stories and applications integrated into each competency to help the reader tie concepts to reality. It is absolutely necessary that test takers apply their knowledge and skills to the test—as well as to life in general. In a friendly, supportive manner, *Passing the Principal TExES Examination* helps test takers and others interested in learner-centered leadership integrate TExES competencies and domains into real-world application. The original 2002 edition became an instant Corwin best seller and remains as such to this day. It is used by universities and alternative preparation programs, as well as individual students, across the state. This second edition continues to be based on domains and competencies provided through Texas law (19 Texas Administrative Code Chapter 241.15) and developed by the Texas State Board for Educator Certification (SBEC) and the success of the original edition. It is written based on the years of experience Wilmore has as a teacher, counselor, principal, professor, and school board member and providing popular, successful, and inspiring TExES preparation seminars at universities, regional service centers, and other training sites around the state. In addition, this updated version also includes updates to the TExES exam and additional test-taking strategies developed since the original printing.

Let's see how.

BASIC CONCEPTS

The principal TExES is divided into three domains with nine competencies. These domains are as follows:

- School community leadership
- Instructional leadership
- Administrative leadership

There are three competencies within school community leadership, four within instructional leadership, and two within administrative leadership. Questions on the test are designed to address specific competencies. They are not evenly divided, however. Approximately 33% of the questions address competencies within school community leadership. Approximately 44% address different competencies from instructional leadership. The final 22% focus on administrative leadership. There is no absolute number of questions per competency or domain. My goal is for *all* my students to get *all* the questions correct, regardless of which domain or competency a question comes from. Nonetheless, a student does not have to score 100% to pass the test. For many students, simply realizing they do not have to earn a perfect score on the test helps to take off some of the pressure, and this is a benefit because half the battle of passing this test is a mind game. In other words, you must know that you can and will succeed. It is my intention for everyone reading this book to win the mind game. You should walk in to take the test feeling cool, calm, collected, confident—and even downright cocky; you should walk out feeling the same. This mental attitude is necessary to lower your level of stress. When your stress level goes up, your productivity goes down (see Figure 1.1). We

Figure 1.1 When Stress Goes Up, Productivity Goes Down

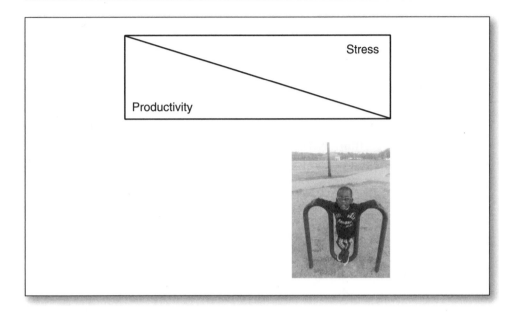

want your stress level down and your productivity to be way up. Therefore, you should be cool, calm, collected, confident, and downright cocky throughout both your preparation and the test-taking experience.

Many people place great emphasis on figuring out exactly which competency each question addresses. Although I discuss this strategy, it does not receive undue attention. Remember, if our goal is to get every question correct, why do we care from which competency the question came? We do not; we want to get all the questions right. Nonetheless, upon becoming thoroughly familiar with each of the competencies, as you will by reading Chapters 3 through 11, you will recognize key words and concepts that will guide your selection of the appropriate answers to get all the questions right—or at least enough questions right to pass.

In addition, there is significant overlap of key themes within the competencies. Since the test is largely a timed mind game, why would you want to get stressed out, with the clock ticking, by worrying if a question is addressing competency 001 or 003? Who cares? The important thing is to understand, integrate, and live the competencies. Make them your "school administrator's bible." Beginning this minute, let your walk match your talk in modeling these competencies in your daily life. Then on the day of the test, walk in there and ace TExES because you are already "walking the talk!"

LEADERSHIP: A SKILL OR AN ART?

There has been, and likely always will be, considerable discussion of whether good leadership is a skill that can be studied or an art that is practiced as diligently as master painters practice their own art form, working hard to produce a masterpiece. For years, researchers such as Kent Peterson, Lee Bolman, and Terrence Deal have presented a view of school leadership that blends concepts of skill and art. Indeed, leadership is a blend of art and skill. Skills are absolutely necessary for good leadership, but they must be practiced and nurtured into the nuances of an art. Never forget that leadership is a talent. Develop it. Nurture it in yourself and in others. Your school, as well as you personally and others whom your leadership affects, will benefit.

Think of leadership as a really good jazz band. As the musicians practice before a performance, they individually sound like a whole lot of noise. They are all doing their own thing, warming up, and getting ready for the concert. But once the performance begins, everything comes together. The musicians play as a team. They are people who have worked hard, practiced together, and who have the common goal of producing really beautiful music. Because they have done those things, the concert begins, and their skills turn into an art as they blend together, bending and flowing with the crescendos and decrescendos, the tempo, and the dynamics of the music to produce something truly beautiful.

Our schools deserve leaders that are orchestrating a wonderful jazz band. As long as everyone in the school is doing their own thing, independent of each other, it is just noise. Although some progress may be made, everyone's skills are acting independently. They are not making beautiful music. But with a great leader—a learner-centered leader with passion, vision, and purpose—the school of musicians can win a Grammy. Every child in every school deserves to be a part of that jazz band, the jazz band that produces artful music, not noise. Every child deserves to be a part of a learning team. Every child deserves to be a part of a school whose staff members are focused on their success in every facet of their lives. Every child deserves the chance to come away a winner.

For too many students today, there is little hope for the future. It is my goal that you become the leader of your school's jazz band. You will be the leader that does what is right instead of what is easy or bureaucratic. You will be the principal that facilitates your school in developing a common vision and a solid purpose built on identified common values. You will be the one to change the world . . . or at least your campus. You will become an awesome principal, or I will come back and haunt you.

But first, you must pass the TExES. Are you ready to get started?

GETTING STARTED

Section II of this book includes Chapters 2 through 11. Chapter 2, "Standing on the Promises," provides the global view of how you will achieve your goal of passing the test. This test is merely a gatekeeper designed to see that you have a specific learner-centered philosophy of school leadership as portrayed in the domains and competencies. It requires entry-level administrative skills and expectations, and it is a passable test. You *will* pass this test.

I teach school leadership at the Texas A&M University at Commerce. I also teach TExES preparation seminars all over the state. It brings me great joy when students from any of them contact me to let me know they passed the test. I get really excited! After all, that means there is one more human out there ready to join my journey toward improving the world. And when you pass, you can send me chocolate (plain Hershey bars, please), roses (I prefer pink), or ice cream (Blue Bell, of course). Chapters 3 through 11 give detailed attention to each of the nine learner-centered competencies. If you have never even heard of them up to this point, that is all right. By the time I get through with you, you will be living and breathing them. If not, you are in a coma. Check with your doctor. It is time to wake up to get ready for this test. You are going to know those competencies inside out. You will be reciting them to your families and friends. If you do not have family or friends, I strongly suggest finding some. They will be a great support system—and they'll be there to celebrate when you pass the test!

Section III addresses the integration and application of all you have learned in Section II. You will become skilled at how to analyze data, learn specific test-taking strategies, create your own Personal Success Plan, and then tie it all together in Section IV, "That's What It's All About." By the time you walk in to take the TExES exam, you will be so well prepared that all you will want to do is go in and pass it so you can go forward to improve the world and eat more chocolate. My goal is to help you pass the test so you can help change the world one school at a time. This test is just a nuisance to get in your way until then. So, let's get rid of the nuisance by passing the test the first time.

Are you ready? Let's go!

SECTION II

Philosophy

The Theoretical Framework

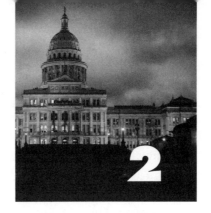

2

Standing on the Promises

GLOBAL OVERVIEW OF TExES DOMAINS

It is helpful to understand "the big picture" of the theoretical framework—that is, the competencies and domains—on which TExES is built before we get into the details of the competencies. As introduced in Chapter 1, the nine competencies are placed into three domains: school community leadership, instructional leadership, and administrative leadership. There is significant overlap in the integration of the individual competencies because a principalship is not a segmented, compartmentalized job. Daily roles and tasks overlap. While fighting the fires of a normal school day, does the average principal stop to ask, "Gee, I wonder if I should respond through Competency 002 or 006?" Definitely not! This is why you should know the competencies inside and out and internalize their concepts so that you can respond reflectively and instinctively. It is not necessary to memorize the competencies. It is necessary to truly understand what they mean. What are the test framers trying to tell you? What they are trying to tell you is what you should look for in potential responses. Pick answers aligned with their philosophy. Give them answers they want to hear.

Before getting into the detailed analysis of the competencies within Chapters 3 through 11, let us discuss specific components in format and the theoretical framework of the domains.

KEY CONCEPTS

I provide three key concepts per domain to help you identify and keep them straight—both as you prepare for the test and afterward as you grow as a principal. These key words will capture the basic essence of what each domain is about. They will help you focus as you dig deeper into the concepts they represent in the competencies. During the test, the concepts they represent will serve as clues to identifying the right answers.

GUESS MY FAVORITES

Each competency chapter features my personal favorites among the domains and competencies. By anticipating ahead of time which ones they are, you will internalize the thought process of the test as well as synthesize what the concepts stand for. It isn't that you really care which my favorites are. This is simply a strategy to help you internalize the philosophy of the test that is necessary for success. During the discussion of the domains in this chapter, I tell you which one is my favorite as a preview to each competency. In Chapters 3 through 11, I don't tell you my favorites until after the discussion. Consider it a game. See if you can figure out which my favorites are before I tell you. If you can, you're off to a great start in that competency. You will also be on your way toward becoming a learner-centered principal. Remember, you may not care what my favorites are. But, you do care about getting the right answers. Guessing my favorites is an excellent tool to assist you in selecting the correct responses.

THE IDEAL PRINCIPAL

For just a few minutes, stop and close your eyes. Visualize in your mind an ideal principal whom you know or with whom you have worked. If you cannot think of an ideal principal, make one up. Perhaps your person will be a combination of the skills or talents of several different principals that you know or wish you knew. Think about all the things this real or imaginary person does or could do. What makes her or him great? What attributes or characteristics does this principal have? What makes the person better than the average principal? What makes this principal outstanding? Take a few minutes to really think about this. *Do not blow off this exercise!*

After you open your eyes, write on a piece of paper the adjectives or other words you used to describe this ideal principal in your mind. Take several minutes to do this. At first, obvious characteristics will come to your mind. Fine. Write them down.

When you think you have thought of them all, dig a little deeper. Come up with some more. It is in this deep reflection that you will get to the heart of the traits of the ideal principal. List 20 to 30. You can do it! Dig deep and come up with some more really good ones. Write them down. From now till eternity, but particularly the day you take the test, you are that principal. You are ideal. Think, breathe, and eat ideal. Be the ideal principal as you pick the ideal responses. Remember, this test is not based on reality. The test designers know you know what reality looks like. They want to know if you know what ideal looks like. The questions are designed to see if you know that. After all, if you don't know what ideal looks like, how are you going to lead a campus toward it?

If possible, prepare for the test with a friend. Study and discuss this book together. Do this exercise together. Then compare your results. Your results will multiply as you collaborate. You will likely have identified many common characteristics, and that's fine. Great principals *do* have many things in common. However, you and your friend may also have come up with different characteristics. Are they things you can agree on? Are they things you both agree constitute this new "mega-ideal principal"? Come up with a master list of characteristics of the ideal principal. Discuss them together. Keep this composite to review periodically before the test. Why did you select these traits and not others? Elaborate on your thought process. This is what becoming a reflective practitioner is all about. This exercise is worth true effort, and it will help you pass the test.

Once you have developed your ideal principal, think about that principal and no other for the rest of your life. Think about that person as you study the domains and competencies. Think about the ideal principal as you select responses to the practice decision set questions at the end of this book. Above all, think only about the ideal principal on the day you take TExES. Do not think, "That's unreasonable," or "That response isn't practical." Forget reasonable and practical! Think ideal! You can be reasonable and practical when you are picking out a new car. On test day, think *ideal principal!* Think, "Dr. Wilmore says, 'Forget reasonable and practical. Think ideal!'" As shown in Figure 2.1, there are enough reasonable and practical principals out there who have totally lost sight of the vision and purpose of the school. Think ideal to change the world—one student and school at a time. Besides, what you learn from this book will haunt you if you ever turn into a bureaucrat.

PRETEND

Remember when you were a child and played pretend games? It was fun to pretend to be an astronaut or president of the United States. (You're never too old to play make-believe!) Well, let's play the pretend game again. Let's say that you are not into this whole "ideal principal" concept.

Figure 2.1 The Ideal Principal Focuses on the Students

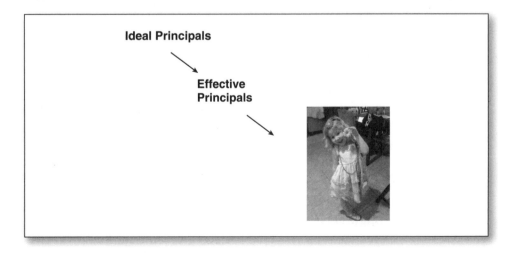

Let's say that thinking "ideal" is just too far-fetched and would never work in the real world. Let's say that you cannot think of a single good reason to hold the ideal principal up as a standard for making TExES exam answer choices.

Pretend. You believe you can become an ideal principal and really affect your school. Imagine how you would feel if this were so. Savor that feeling and work toward it forever.

There is no law that says you have to believe in any of the traits of the ideal principal. Maybe your goal in life is to be a bureaucrat. If this is true, I have suggestions:

1. On the day of the test, pretend like crazy! You may not buy the philosophy of the ideal principal, but I can guarantee one thing. The developers of this test do, and they hold all the cards. Therefore, if you want to pass this test, pretend like crazy.

2. What if you can't do it? You simply do not buy one word of this "ideal principal" concept. You really do want to become a bureaucrat. You have a burning desire to sit in the principal's office listening to Mozart, doing as little as possible, and never actually become invested in the lives of others. Nonetheless, you'd like to look important while you do nothing. Here's my suggestion. Put away this book. It will do nothing for you except raise your blood pressure.

You've learned the way you're supposed to think to pass this test and change the world, and you've learned to pretend on test day—that is, if you have difficulty with the concept of the ideal principal. Now it's time to get started with the three domains.

Important Recurring Themes and Concepts: The Sherrys

It can be overwhelming to look at the entire Principal TExES Preparation Manual and see all those pages of domains, competencies, and practice decision sets. However, it is not nearly as daunting as it may seem. The test developers actually have some favorite concepts and use them over and over. They simply spin them different directions within each of the three domains.

Think of it this way. If a new set of parents name their baby "Sherry" and "Sherry" is not a family name, we can assume they must like the name Sherry. The same is true with this TExES exam. There are themes and concepts that the domains and competencies use over and over. We will call them our Sherrys. Just as new parents must like a name or they would not have picked it, the same will be true for us. Once we identify the Sherrys when we see them in answer options, we realize they are there for a reason. The test developers like them. They are the test Sherrys. Pick and use them accordingly. A sampling of Sherrys appears in Figure 2.2, Important Recurring Themes and Concepts: The "Sherry" List. Watch for the Sherrys in Chapters 3 through 11, see if you can identify more, and be particularly vigilant to watch for them as you take the actual examination.

Figure 2.2 Important Recurring Themes and Concepts: The "Sherry" List

• All	• Professional development
• Alignment	• Enhancing everything: How can I make It better?
• Collaborate	• Ongoing, continuous assessment
• Data-based decisions	• Multiple and diverse forms of assessment and measurement
• The 1–2–3–4 Plan	• High expectations
• Develop—create—design	• Facilitate
• Articulate—communicate—market	• Student advocate
• Implement—put into action	• Student needs
• Evaluate—assess	• Participatory leadership and management
• Culture	
• Climate	
• Vision	
• Lifelong learning	

THE THREE DOMAINS

Domain I: School Community Leadership

Key Words: Culture, Climate, and Vision

Domain I is *school community leadership.* Approximately 33% of the test is from this domain. I love this domain. It is my personal favorite. It likely will not take you long to figure out why.

Figure 2.3 The Nine Domain Competencies Focus on Student Success

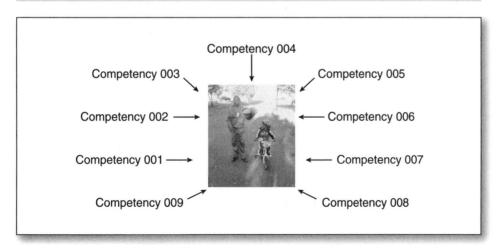

Competency 004

Competency 003

Competency 005

Competency 002

Competency 006

Competency 001

Competency 007

Competency 009

Competency 008

In a nutshell, school community leadership concentrates on all the things a principal should do to develop and nurture a culture, climate, and vision of the school whose staff members are supportive of all stakeholders and help them succeed. Who is a stakeholder? Everyone. Absolutely no one is left out. Stakeholders go hand-in-hand with another key TExES term and concept: the *learning community* or *school community*. The idea is to get everyone possible involved in identifying common values, developing a shared purpose and vision of the school, and developing goals and strategies to achieve them. The school community consists of teachers, counselors, paraprofessionals, auxiliary personnel, parents, community members, businesses, churches, and everyone else interested in the school. The more people you can get involved, the better. People support what they help build. Our schools need all the help and support they can get.

You may ask, "What if my school is simply awful? What if it is located in a part of town where no one wants to go? It is dangerous. The idea of getting parents or anyone else involved is pretty far-fetched." Fine. Think far-fetched. Remember, we are focused on the ideal principal. The ideal principal learned at the feet of Winston Churchill. During the bleakest moments of World War II, Churchill was known for telling the English that their nation would never, never give up. England never did give up. Eventually, the Allies won the war, preserving freedom and democracy for the next generation. It did not happen by taking the easy road or rolling over and playing dead. It happened through hard work, perseverance, and collaboration with other countries.

The same is true within Domain I. The ideal principal will never give up. It doesn't matter how bleak the circumstances; ideal principals pick themselves up, dust themselves off, and start all over again. They ask themselves, "How can I do this better next time?" Why do they ask themselves that? Because there is *always* a next time. Therefore, we need to make every unsuccessful venture a learning opportunity. Either we grow and learn from our mistakes or we keep making the same ones over and over. That's called settling for the status quo.

The ideal principal abhors the status quo. The ideal principal is always striving to make every single thing better. Making every single thing better is how we move toward ideal.

It takes intense resiliency to be a great school principal. Anyone can be a lackluster, status quo principal. Who on Earth needs more of those? Certainly not us! We are Domain I principals, intent on facilitating so that everyone collaborates for a better tomorrow. It's a vision thing. Never give up. Never.

Can you see why this domain is my favorite?

Domain II: Instructional Leadership

Key Words: Curriculum, Instruction, and Staff Development

Domain II is the "meat and potatoes" of the principalship. It is what makes us different from chief executive officers or managers of any other organization. We are here to lead schools, not shoe stores. What are we selling? Curriculum and instruction. How do we do that? Through improved staff development. Notice, I did not say *teacher* development. That would be limiting. As lifelong learners we believe in developing and nurturing *all* people—that includes *everyone* at the school and beyond. We do not want to limit anything or anyone. Motivational speaker Les Brown says to reach for the moon. Even if you do not reach it, you will land among the stars. Awesome principals want to nurture and develop everyone. They reach for the moon and settle for the stars only if they have to. Landing among the stars sure beats being in the pits, however.

Always dream big. I tell my students that if they do not remember one other thing that I teach them, to remember to dream big dreams. I even have it on my voice mail. You would be surprised how many people leave messages commenting about what a surprise it is to hear anyone encouraging them to "dream big." I always wonder, isn't dreaming big what universities are all about?

In fact, isn't that what all schools are for? Domain II is about improving curriculum and instruction for the benefit of all students. It's about finding ways to nurture and develop staff members so they can be the arms and legs for improved curriculum and instruction, to meet the developmental needs of all students.

This would be a good time to introduce the Texas Assessment of Knowledge and Skills (TAKS) and the State of Texas Assessments of Academic Readiness, commonly called STAAR.

STAAR, and TAKS before it, begin in the third grade and continue through Grade 8. It was originally given primarily in reading, math, and writing with secondary schools also reporting End-of-Course (EOC) test results. Subsequently, tests in both science and social studies were added. Some subjects, such as writing, science, and social studies, are not given in every grade; thus, there will not be any scores reported for the grades in which they are not given. Currently, STAAR is not given on the secondary level. Secondary EOC exams are currently given in 12 areas. These are English I, English II, English III, Algebra I, Algebra II, Geography, World Geography, World History, U.S. History, Biology, Chemistry, and Physics. Test results are reported in Section I because all testing information is in Section I, regardless if it is elementary or secondary.

For out-of-state test takers, STAAR and the EOCs are really big tests in Texas. Students begin taking it in the third grade. They keep taking it until they pass the high school version. If students do not pass the high school TAKS, they do not graduate, period. It doesn't matter if they make straight A's. It doesn't matter how many honors or advanced placement classes they have taken. It doesn't matter if they have a wonderful scholarship waiting for them. They must pass that test. Students who fail STAAR in the early grades are identified as "at risk." Plans are made to remediate them so they will pass the following year, to help get them on track for the high school exam. The public schools of Texas are under intense pressure for students to do well on both STAAR and the EOCs. The state accountability system is directly linked to student success or failure on them. The TExES refers to TAKS, because it was around so long, and now STAAR and EOCs many times. It is not the purpose of this book to address whether this high-stakes testing is a good thing or a bad thing. It doesn't matter—it's the law. And if it's the law, then it's the hand we're dealt. And if it's the hand we're playing, you can guess what we must do. *Win!*

If we think of state exams as important games that we intend to win, we must become coaches and produce game plans and strategies to make sure we do. How many coaches do you know that say, "Well, guys, it's Friday night in Texas. Half the town will be out there waiting to see you play. They don't really care if you win or lose. They just want to see you looking good in those great uniforms." Right. In *Texas?* I don't think so. In Texas, teams are expected to win. If they do not, serious things can happen. It is downright unTexan!

Domain II is about winning. Think "curriculum, instruction, and staff development." Our tools for winning are curriculum, instruction, and staff development. They are our game plan. They are the "meat and potatoes" of who we are and why we are here. To create a better world, we must have an educated society. Meat and potatoes. Curriculum, instruction, and staff development. Domain II. Think winning!

Domain III: Administrative Leadership

Key Words: Resources, Facilities, and Safety

The third domain, administrative leadership, is different from the first two. Domain I deals with the culture, climate, and vision of the school. Domain II deals with the "meat and potatoes," the staples of schooling that are curriculum, instruction, and staff development. Domain III takes a slightly different direction. It deals with the business of managing the school. It is absolutely necessary that principals are committed and passionate about the campus vision and that they do everything possible to augment appropriate curriculum and instruction. Still, if principals cannot appropriately manage the daily operations of their schools, ultimately they will not be successful.

Domain III deals with budget, resource allocation, financial management, personnel management, facilities, and safety. For principals to be effective, they must provide a balance of leadership and management skills. It won't matter if you are passionate about meeting the needs of all students if you cannot plan for and allocate funds properly. Your central business office will take action if you continually run with a deficit. They may be kind about it once or twice, but if the problem continues, they will not be so understanding. If you do not get your act together, upper administration will see to it that you don't have that problem anymore because you will no longer be the principal. This will not help the cause of proactive change agents, so Domain III is very important.

There is one specific aspect of Domain III that bears emphasis here, as well as within subsequent chapters. That is the issue of school safety. We used to think of school safety as having a safe facility, with access for the disabled, safe playgrounds, and the right number of fire, tornado, or other emergency drills. Unfortunately, our world has moved far beyond that with out of control violence and bullying. With school shootings brought to national attention from the horrible deaths at Columbine High School in Colorado violence has infiltrated one of the most sacred institutions in the United States: where we educate our young. This is wrong, and there is no way to justify it.

But violence is also reality. To ignore the fact that it occurs would be to hide our heads in the sand. Positive, change-agent principals never hide their heads in the sand. They are always looking ahead by having practiced emergency plans in place. Furthermore, in their proactivity these principals are constantly vigilant of signs that students or others are in need, and they work to meet those needs so that a school's emergency plans will never be put into action.

The ideal principal never gives up. The ideal principal works constantly, without letting up, to maintain a safe and effective learning environment for all students. Anything less is simply going through the motions.

You have now been introduced to the global view of the three learner-centered domains. The next nine chapters delve into the specificity of the nine competencies that fall within these three domains. From the beginning you will know that if a competency—or a test question—has something to do with vision, climate, or culture, it is likely a Domain I question. You should look for a test response that also directly relates to the same issue. The same is true for the other two domains. To keep your domains straight, remember your key concepts.

Remember as well that sometimes the TExES provides what seems to be an excellent answer choice but that doesn't answer the question to which it refers. If you are nervous and see an answer choice that says, "George Washington was the first President of the United States," you may think, "That's right!" But, remember, the question had nothing to do with George Washington. A nervous mind can play tricks on you so beware. Make sure you pick the answer that is aligned with this specific question. Underline important words in the prompt and question to keep you focused on exactly what is asked. If the test gives you a wonderful selection choice, but it doesn't apply to the question and isn't in line with the appropriate domain, forget it. It may be beautiful, but it isn't the right answer to the question. Now let's take a look at those nine competencies.

Learner-Centered Leadership and Campus Culture

Domain I: Leadership of the Educational Community

Domain Key Concepts: Campus Culture, Climate, and Vision

Competency 001

The principal knows how to shape school culture by facilitating the development, articulation, implementation, and stewardship of a vision of learning that is shared and supported by the educational community.

A case could easily be made that 001 is the most important competency of them all. If you understand and are able to apply it, almost everything in the other eight competencies will fall under this umbrella. This competency is all about the school vision. Everything we do, say, or research should be something that is going to facilitate obtaining the school vision. Therefore, it is of utmost importance that the entire school community work together to determine exactly what the school vision is or should be, what is needed to achieve it, and how it will be articulated, measured, and, if necessary, modified. The school vision should briefly summarize everything the school hopes their students will know, be able to do, and exemplify. It includes the knowledge base, skills, and attitudes necessary to becoming a productive citizen. It is the master plan into which campus and departmental goals feed.

Altogether, every school campus, department, and function should have its own vision, its own goals, and its own strategies for attainment, measurement, and, if necessary, revision. Obtaining the vision is what everything we do every day is all about. If, based upon a needs assessment and an audit of how time in classrooms is actually being spent, it is determined that things are occurring that do not support the vision, they are a

Figure 3.1 All Campus and Department Goals Should Be Student Focused

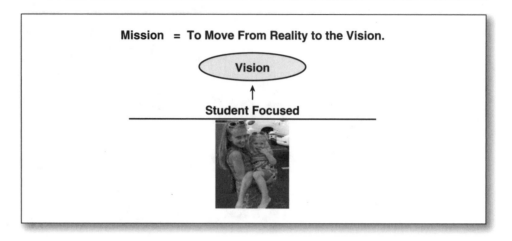

waste of time and should be eliminated. No school time should be spent on anything that does not move the school toward attainment of a specific goal and, thus, the campus vision.

The vision is the single most important element that the principal should lead the school, both macroscopically and microscopically, into developing, articulating, and using. It is the purpose for which the school exists.

What is your school vision? What steps are being taken to achieve it, if any? If the answers to these questions do not come immediately to your mind, you have serious work ahead. Without a clearly articulated vision, the school is approaching education by a shotgun approach, where pellets/actions are flying everywhere, instead of a rifle approach, where the concept is clearly focused upon a specific target. It is time we as schools start

Figure 3.2 Vision–Goal–Daily-Activities Alignment

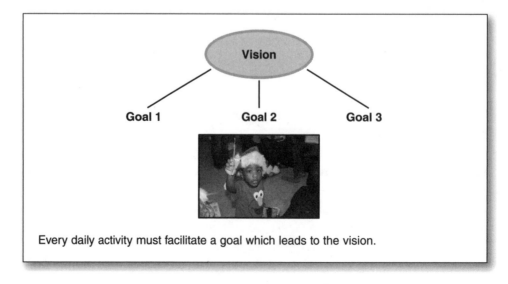

Figure 3.3 Competency–Based Principals Are Visionaries

- Develop a campus vision.

- Articulate the campus vision.

- Implement the campus vision.

- Be good stewards of the campus vision.

The vision is the tool that highly successful principals use to guide the campus to optimum success. The importance of the vision cannot be overstated.

working smarter rather than harder. The school vision is the tool by which this can occur.

This competency is so important that before we get into any examples of principal performance, I want to walk you through it virtually word by word. There is so much packed into this short sentence that I am afraid you will miss something if I don't make sure you get it piece by piece, bit by bit.

The competency begins with, "The principal know how to *shape* school culture . . . " It does not say the principal comes in and immediately tells everyone what the culture will be, how it will be developed or nourished, or even how it will be measured. It says the principal shapes the school culture. This is important because of what the verb *shape* says. It is not autocratic. It is collaborative with the interest and input of the entire school community being highly involved in its development, articulation, and implementation. So, watch for questions that have answers that come from an autocratic, top-down perspective. They are wrong answers. Watch for answers that show the principal as shaping what is going on. Those are the correct answers.

As principal, your primary role is to be a *facilitator.* It is not your job to do everything. That's what you have other people for. However, it is your job to facilitate in order to ensure that everything gets done. Therefore, when you are shaping everything from the vision to learner-centered objectives or bond elections, you are leading as a facilitator. From the perspective of this test, that is a good thing. You are not heavy-handed. You are not a dictator. You are a facilitator, working with the input of virtually everyone to reach collaborative decisions together. Thus, you are shaping the school culture rather than defining it exclusively from your own perceptions and views. Thus, you are a principal who "knows how to shape school culture by *facilitating* . . ." in truth, virtually everything.

Now let's talk about what I call the 1–2–3–4 Plan shown here in Figure 3.4.

Go back to the competency itself. Take your pencil and mark 1 by *development*, 2 by *articulation*, 3 by *implementation,* and 4 by *stewardship of a vision of learning*. As shown in Figure 3.4, we are numbering them 1–2–3–4 because that is the order they are given to us. Why is that such a big deal?

There are several reasons. Throughout the test, there will be multiple times when you are asked which of the following things the principal would do "first" or "initially." While all of the items may look good, before answering, go back to your 1–2–3–4 Plan. Ask yourself, which one of these things goes with Number 1, which is *developing*? What other words could they possibly use that are synonyms for *developing*? Make yourself a list right now so that when you see any of those words on the test, you will recognize them as meaning the same thing as *developing*. Some choices include

- planning,
- designing,
- creating,
- building,
- expanding, and
- growing.

It is important to utilize good planning first, because we do not want to put the cart in front of the ox. For example, a good contractor does not simply start building a school without first studying the previously developed architectural designs to know how the school is supposed to look when it is finished. The *details* of the construction have already been worked out as part of this planning process. Stephen Covey (1990) told us to begin with the end in mind. That's what we are doing when we work collaboratively with others. We accomplish this developmental planning process first through developing or enhancing a school culture in Domain I, by improving and aligning the curriculum with developmentally appropriate instructional techniques in Domain II, and by facilitating a school budget based on student needs in Domain III. It makes no difference what the issue, domain, or competency is. First, or initially, important collaborative planning must take place. We do not reach conclusions by seat of the pants techniques or make long-term decisions by what is most popular at the

Figure 3.4

1. Develop—Create—Design—Plan

2. Articulate—Communicate—Market

3. Implement—To Put the Design Into Action

4. Steward (Nurture, Sustain) or Evaluate—Measure—Assess

moment. Instead, good principals involve others, research and analyze data, and subsequently develop plans for the issue based on accurate information rather than perception. That is why the first element in the 1–2–3–4 Plan is so important and why I am putting such attention on it right here in the beginning. Remember it throughout all 10 competencies.

The next element in the 1–2–3–4 Plan is *articulation*. To articulate something means to communicate whatever it is in a way that other people can understand. This goes beyond being a language issue even though that is certainly extremely important. As educators we have a tendency to talk in our own jargon (some people call it "educationese") that others cannot comprehend. Anything we say to the community, to teachers, to parents, or to whoever, must be done in a way that they clearly understand and are able to comprehend. They may not agree with us, but at least they understand what it is we are trying to get across and the rationale upon which it is based. Therefore, whether we are articulating the school culture in Domain I, new curriculum or teacher assessment in Domain II, or a crisis management plan in Domain III, it is important that it is done in a way that people can understand. Remember, you cannot clearly articulate something until after it is developed. That is why *articulation* is Number 2, whereas *development* is Number 1.

Take a minute to brainstorm other words that the test developers could use in questions instead of the word *articulate* but which mean the same thing. This is important because it is likely what they will do. Some words they may use are

- communicate,
- explain,
- elaborate,
- define,
- discuss, and
- market.

The exact word they use is not the issue. It is the *concept* of making sure you understand it is our job to clearly communicate everything that is going on in the school to all stakeholders. People cannot support what they do not know or understand.

The next step in the 1–2–3–4 Plan is *implementation*. We cannot implement, or put into place, anything *appropriately* unless it has been properly developed and communicated to all stakeholders. Therefore, to maximize our school productivity, before putting any new program into action, or after working to improve an existing function, we first put great effort into developing it properly by using current research and data and then ensuring that all stakeholders know what we are doing, how it was developed, why it is important, how it will be assessed, and what their roles are. After *all* of that has been done, we actually implement whatever it is we have been working toward. It is important that we keep all of these things in the right order. Do not skip steps. If, in an effort to save time, we skimp on any step, or simply skip it, the results will manifest themselves in the lack of *maximized* success in the implementation. In today's schools, we do not have time for anything less than *maximized* success, so do not skip or skimp on steps in the 1–2–3–4 Plan. You will reap what you sow.

Think about other words or phrases that the test developers could use instead of implementation. Some could include

- strategies,
- techniques,
- action plans,
- putting something in place,
- starting a new program or curriculum,
- enhancing an existing program or curriculum, and
- just doing it.

The last element in the 1–2–3–4 Plan is *stewardship of a vision of learning*. Everything we do should be assessed. A retired Navy admiral once said, "What gets measured gets done." But the *stewardship* of the vision goes beyond assessment and measurement to the nurturing, sustaining, enrichment, and refinement of whatever it is we have been working so hard on in Steps 1, 2, and 3. This is the building up of our people when they are tired. It is the lifting up and encouragement of teachers and support personnel as they are pressured and stressed beyond all measure at state testing times. It is being the school shepherd who takes care, nurtures, and sustains everyone toward their roles in the development, articulation, implementation, and refinement of the vision. It is a very important component because it pulls the first three together. It is also the one that is least likely to actually take place in a consistent, systems-approach manner. We need to take care of each other. If we do not take care of our principals and teachers, they can eventually become so tired, so "soul fatigued" (Wilmore, 2007) that they can no longer come close to working at peak performance.

Being an educator is a calling. Being a principal is a special calling. Principals are more than business managers (Domain III) or instructional specialists (Domain II). Principals are the role models of professionalism in creating a school culture that values a collaboratively developed vision. Figure 3.5 shows the distinction between reality (where we are now) and the school vision (where we want to be). Our mission, thus, is to move us from reality to the vision. Saying this may sound easy. Accomplishing it is definitely not.

This "vision of learning" will be "shared and supported by the educational community" when it is developed with everyone working together toward a common goal of success for all students regardless of who they are, what their race, religion, gender, mobility, financial status, or demographics are. Unfortunately, not everyone agrees on everything all the time. Figure 3.6 illustrates that all people do not hold the same views and belief systems. Our goal is to seek, find, and utilize even the smallest area of common ground as a starting point for creating the school vision and everything else.

Figure 3.5 Vision and Goal Setting Alignment: All Goals Should Support the District Vision to Move the School From Reality to the Vision

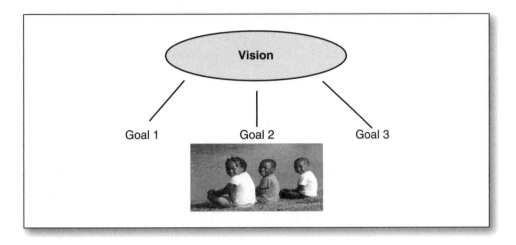

Figure 3.6 Identifying and Respecting the Common Ground

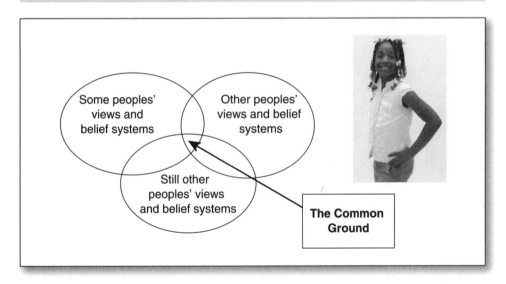

Dr. Jesse Jai McNeil, Jr., founder and president of the McNeil Ecumenical Leadership Foundation, says people support what they help create. It is true. This competency is all about getting everyone to work together to develop a vision and goals that they subsequently share and support, because they developed them together. World peace may sound like something contestants in beauty pageants say they are hoping to achieve. I hope they do. But there will likely be more to it than a pretty smile. However, educators working together with their communities do have a real chance of making an impact on society and peace one school at a time. That is what this competency is all about. I love it. It is my very favorite. I hope it will be yours too. If you can nail this one, you can nail the test. Everything else fits under this umbrella of vision.

Go forth, determine your personal vision, plan the goals and steps you will need to take to achieve it, and go do it. Do not sit around wishing any more. Get something done! The difference between success and failure is that one lets adversity get in its way, while the other climbs over adversity to make the world a better place. *That* is the principal I want you to be. As you are answering the test questions, make *sure* you are that principal!

Other words or phrases that test preparers could use instead of stewardship

- nurturing,
- sustaining,
- enriching,
- advocating,
- supporting, and
- measuring and assessing for improvement.

THE PRINCIPAL KNOWS HOW TO . . .

- *Create a school culture that sets high expectations, promotes learning, and provides intellectual stimulation for self, students, and staff members.*

It is one thing to say you promote learning, high expectations, and academic rigors for yourself, students, and staff, but what are you doing that shows it? It must be more than simply talking about it. It must be doing it on a daily basis. Your walk must match your talk. Test questions are constructed to see if you realize these things are important by the choices you make.

Please make sure you notice that this competency also holds you to these same high expectations for continuing your own learning, maintaining high expectations for your own performance, and exhibiting rigor in everything you do. Beware of questions that are embedded with the expectation that these issues apply to you as well.

- *Respond appropriately to diverse needs in shaping the campus culture.*

This one is nothing short of beautiful. In fact, it is almost poetic in its beauty. Positive, proactive principals know this and respond appropriately to the diverse needs of different subgroups of students, parents, faculty, staff members, and the school community—in other words, they respond to the needs of *all* stakeholders. Everyone, and everything that happens, is a part of the campus culture. Students live, learn, and react differently. So does everyone else. Today's world is more diverse than any time in the past and growing more diverse daily. Do not avoid the change. Be ready for it. Embrace it. Respond appropriately to it. The future of our democratic society depends on it.

The principal is not just the CEO of the school. The principal's values and dispositions set the culture and climate for the entire campus.

Therefore, it is of critical importance that you do everything within your capabilities to promote multicultural awareness: that all of us live in the same society together; thus, it is the responsibility of all of us to get to know, understand, and promote cultures other than our own.

The same is equally true of gender sensitivity. Each person, regardless of his or her sex, is of equal value and must have equal opportunities for academic, athletic, social, extra- and co-curricular, and leadership opportunities. Within classrooms, every occasion must be utilized to meet the needs of all students regardless of their gender, race, or socioeconomic status. Equity continues to be an issue.

Last, there is greater diversity in classrooms and communities than there has been in our history. Remember, diversity is not limited to race. It includes gender, race, mobility, culture, socioeconomics, and so forth. Very important, students also have different learning styles, for which there must be adaptations. It is not the responsibility of the students to change their learning styles to make life easier on educators. It is our responsibility to change our teaching and leading styles to best meet their needs. Sometimes it seems like we get that backward. In the schools you lead, make sure everyone knows, understands, and appreciates equity, sensitivity, and the value of diversity.

- *Use various types of information (e.g., demographic data, campus climate inventory results, student achievement data, emerging issues affecting education) to develop a campus vision and create a plan for implementing the vision.*

There is a concept called triangulation that you may remember from your research classes. Triangulation simply means using multiple sources of data to gather input, verify results, and draw appropriate conclusions. This is called data-driven decision making. The test developers love decisions that are based on data. As an ideal principal, you will make all of your decisions based on data rather than what is easy to do or what others want you to do.

In this instance, the various types of information, with examples provided, should be used to develop a campus vision and create a plan for implementing the vision. As we have discussed repeatedly, the development, articulation, implementation, and stewardship of the campus vision is absolutely essential to campus success. It is the common denominator of everything we do. It must be our daily focus. If it isn't, we are not moving toward ideal. The vision is where we look when we are discouraged. It is there to lift us up, to refocus us on where we are as well as where we want to be. Without a clearly defined and articulated campus vision, we are not what we should be, which is a definite disservice to our school community. If we take our eyes off the vision and are unable or unwilling to refocus, it is time to make a decision. Either refocus or leave education completely. Our students deserve principals who are 100% committed to the campus vision and who will move Heaven and earth to see that it is obtained.

Further, you must facilitate the creation of a plan for communicating, implementing, and evaluating the vision. How is this done? It is accomplished through collaborative collegial relationships with all members of the school community. Again, this is not something that can be done or thrown together quickly in an after-school faculty meeting. It takes time, deep concentration, and continuous analysis of every kind of data you can get your hands on. In Chapter 12, "No Data Left Behind," we discuss this in more detail. In simple but firm language, every school must have a strong vision and a plan on exactly how to get to it. Pretty words on paper are not enough. Daily action is required.

- *Use strategies for involving all stakeholders in planning processes to enable the collaborative development of a shared campus vision focused on teaching and learning.*

Exactly how are you going to involve all stakeholders, including those whose opinions and philosophies are different from yours, for planning on school issues? How are you going to be the one to facilitate this design between different constituencies or groups? While it is true that you will have a staff to help with these things, in the end, it will fall on you. You are the leader of the school. You are the one who will set the stage, the expectations, and will facilitate the campus culture and climate to ensure that appropriate planning occurs and that people from all walks of life are integrally included. Value the contributions of others, particularly those from the school community. Test questions will not ask you to specify what actions you would take in reality. However, they will ask you to select appropriate responses regarding how you would react in fictitious ones. Therefore, as you are reading and selecting the correct response, remember to look for the response that includes *all* stakeholders and where you act as the facilitator between diverse groups. Some of these groups may not agree or even like each other. It will be your role to walk that fine line of problem solver in group-planning processes. It is your job to bring varying opinions to a common core that everyone can commit to and work toward.

It is a heavy responsibility. Are you ready for it?

- *Facilitate the collaborative development of a plan that clearly articulates objectives and strategies for implementing a campus vision.*

As we have discussed, collaboratively developing, articulating, and implementing a shared vision that focuses on teaching and learning is what the role of the principal is all about. The reason we keep coming back to it is to reinforce exactly how important it is. Communicating the vision, as well as exactly how the campus plan will help you reach it, is what you do all day, every day. Figure 3.7 demonstrates how all school goals must support, be aligned with, and lead to the school vision. All of the school community must understand the rationale of the vision and how and why it was created, and it must be clearly communicated with all stakeholders

Figure 3.7 Campus Activities Should Be Clearly Articulated to the District Vision

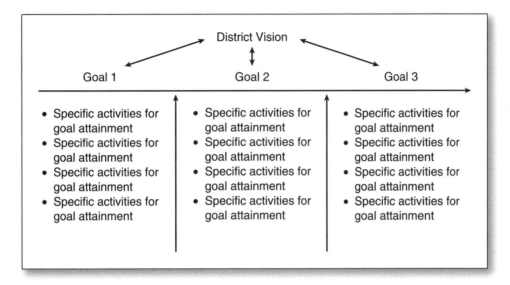

to ensure they understand it. No one can truly support something they do not totally understand.

Similarly, Figure 3.7 further shows how all school activities should lead to the success of a targeted goal while all goals continue to lead to attainment of the school vision.

Everything the school does should be about ensuring, or guaranteeing, that all students are successful. This includes those students with emotional issues, those who move a lot, those who are discipline problems, those who may not have enough to eat or wear, those with learning disabilities, and those whose first language may not remotely resemble English. "All students" means every single one of them. Exactly what will you as principal do to ensure the success for each of these students? These are the issues the questions will address. Make sure your responses do not exclude anyone but look to benefit every student.

It isn't easy to develop and maintain a positive school climate that can be used for effective and responsible decision making. So, how will you do this on a regular basis? Is it enough to keep your eyes and ears open to virtually everything that comes up? How will you monitor and assess the climate? In fact, exactly how would you differentiate between formal and informal techniques for doing exactly that?

The key to passing this test is not only to understand the competencies but also to know how to apply them. In anticipation of that, develop

- three techniques to monitor and assess school climate, and

- a depiction of a situation you have experienced (or one you have made up) in which monitoring and assessing school climate for effective, responsive decision making was utilized. Describe how you, as the ideal principal, could have handled it in a different and more productive manner.

> • *Align financial, human, and material resources to support implementation of a common vision.*

The concept of "align, alignment, aligns, or aligned" is one of the test developers' favorite Sherrys. It comes up repeatedly throughout the competencies. You will definitely see it in questions and responses on the test. You must really understand what it means to be able to apply it. In simple terms, it means everything goes together or matches. Are your daily activities things that will help your campus accomplish goals that will help you reach your vision? If not, they are not aligned. If you say you need specific resources to implement strategies for goal attainment, they must be in the budget. If not, your budget is not aligned with your goals and vision.

As shown in Figure 3.8 all financial, human, and material resources necessary must be aligned to support the campus vision.

It is important that you understand that it is the responsibility of the principal to make sure there are procedures for monitoring the accomplishment of school goals and objectives to achieve the school's vision. Consider the efficacy of these issues:

• Are our goals directly aligned with our vision to meet the needs of every student?

• How will we monitor and measure student accomplishment?

• If everything we do is to help the school achieve its goals and objectives to achieve the vision, exactly what will you as a principal do to assess these things? Once the assessments are in place, how will you utilize the results? What potential changes can take place based on the data-driven results?

Figure 3.8   Budget-Vision Alignment

Budget ⟶ Resources ⟶ Strategies ⟶ Goals ⟶ Vision

It is actually a very linear process. As previously shown in Figure 3.6, the vision should have multiple goals and objectives to support it. If it doesn't, it is meaningless rhetoric. Each goal and objective should subsequently have specific activities and strategies that will ensure they are achieved. Each activity or strategy should have

- a timeline for accomplishment;

- a mechanism by which it will be assessed;

- a process, based on assessment results, by which strategies can be modified or edited to better facilitate goal attainment;

- specific resources that are necessary to accomplish the activity or strategy; and

- plans for staff development necessary to facilitate the attainment of goals that are included in the budget.

Remember, it does not matter how good an action plan looks or sounds. What matters is student learning. No matter how much work and effort has gone into planning something, if assessment shows it is not working or it is not maximizing productivity, it is time to make changes. In order to reach the school's vision, many changes in the way things are done and taught will likely have to occur. Change is a necessary part of the improvement process. It is also necessary to take the school from where it is to where it wants to be. In so doing, we are enhancing the quality of education for every student.

- *Establish procedures to access and modify implementation plans to ensure achievement of the campus vision.*

Figure 3.9 Improving the Process for Greater Student Achievement

Enhancing Education = Making Lives Better.

Resource procurement and management skills are essential strategies every principal must have to facilitate the school reaching its vision. In so doing, we must align the things identified as necessary to reach determined goals and objectives. This skill includes having the right people in the appropriate roles to access and modify virtually everything to enhance student learning. It is very difficult, and often impossible, to reach a goal without the necessary people and resources. Therefore, for the school financial plan to be aligned with its vision, all necessary materials, equipment, and personnel must be budgeted for and used in a judicious manner as previously shown in Figure 3.7.

- *Support innovative thinking and risk taking within the school community and view unsuccessful experiences as learning opportunities.*

School improvement necessitates change. The Seven Last Words of a Decaying School are, "We never did it that way before." Change precipitates improvement. Without change, we will keep getting what we have always got. If that is good enough for you, shame on you. We are here to be change agents and to make sure that every student has the best chance possible to receive a free and appropriate education. We can't do that by continuing to operate the way we have always done things, holding steadfastly to the status quo. Ask yourself, is what we are accomplishing good enough? If not, don't just sit there laissez-faire. Do something about it!

A proactive, change-oriented principal displays data-based innovative thinking and risk taking on a regular basis while also encouraging others to do likewise. This innovative thinking and risk taking is what will bring about positive change and school improvement. That is what we are all about.

But what happens when a new endeavor is planned, articulated, and implemented (do you recognize the 1–2–3–4 Plan here?), yet it does not turn out well? In fact, it turns into a great big bust. Virtually nothing about it went right.

In those cases, none feel worse than those who are directly involved. They know a bust when they see one. If you come down on them when they are already down, they will never get over it or forget it. In essence, you kicked them when they were down. Who likes that?

Yet the situation cannot be ignored either. What you want to do is turn it into a learning opportunity. Utilize the firm arm with the velvet glove. Talk to those involved from a mentoring perspective. Discuss the situation in a nonthreatening manner. Brainstorm what went wrong, possible causes, and ways a similar disaster could be averted in the future. In essence, use your firm arm to have those involved think it through and brainstorm ways to improve the situation should something similar arise in the future. In this way, you have turned a problem into a learning opportunity. You have turned a bad situation into a great example of the principal in a teaching and learning moment. Those are the most gratifying of all. By not being condescending, but approaching it in a firm but helpful manner, you have turned what could have been a relationship

Figure 3.10 Turn Obstacles Into Student-Focused Learning Opportunities

spoiler into one that builds trust and unity toward the school vision. That is what being an educational leader is about.

- *Acknowledge and celebrate the contributions of students, staff members, parents, and community toward realization of the school's vision.*

In supervisory roles, unfortunately it seems human nature to come down on people when they do something wrong. Sometimes corrective feedback is provided. Too often it isn't. Yet it is much rarer to give enough kudos, publicly and privately, when things go right, when someone accomplishes something that was almost impossible, or when a goal is reached that is very rare or unique. In those cases, it is very important to the school culture and climate, as well as vision attainment, for you both to recognize these people's efforts and to celebrate them publicly. The same congratulatory manner should also be given to the community when it has come through on a difficult issue, particularly one that involves potentially raising taxes such as through a bond issue. Another example of celebration should be when solid test scores come in. Everyone should be lauded with more than a onetime, "Gee, fifth-grade reading scores really came up this year. You must have worked really hard." Let your pride in the efforts of campuses, students, families, and the community really show. Let them feel your pride in their accomplishments.

What they have done may not be as big a deal as improved test scores. They could be little things like teachers coming early and staying late to tutor students for no additional pay. That is laudatory behavior and happens very often. There are people who routinely go the extra mile, then another extra mile, to help students have a decent life. Just the right word from you to let them know that you are aware of what they have done, or are doing, can mean so much. When you touch a heart, you touch a life. Celebrate with people when they are happy or have received a blessing. Have empathy with them when they are down. When you do these things, they will come back to you in deepened relationships, trust, and team building toward the school's goals and vision.

GUESS MY FAVORITES

It's all about the vision. The vision is everything. Part of that vision is establishing and supporting the school culture. All of this starts at the top with the principal.

- *Create a campus culture that sets high expectations, promotes learning, and provides intellectual stimulation for self, students, and staff members.*
- *Support innovative thinking and risk taking within the school community and view unsuccessful experiences as learning opportunities.*
- *Acknowledge and celebrate the contributions of students, staff members, parents, and community members toward realization of the campus vision.*

IMPORTANT POINTS TO REMEMBER

- It is all about the vision. If something does not relate to the vision, do not waste your time with it.
- Use the 1–2–3–4 Plan.
     Utilize the 1–2–3–4 Plan in order. It is not the 3–1–2–4 Plan. It is called the 1–2–3–4 Plan for a reason. Remember that for all questions.
- Collaborate with everyone.
- Diversity is important. Everyone is important.
- The educational community consists of everyone.
- People support what they help create.
- Support, encourage, and sustain your people.
- Everyone can be successful when provided with the right support.
- Formally and informally assess everything all the time for the purpose of making it better.
- Be active and informed professionally.

4

Learner-Centered Communication and Community Relations

Domain I: School Community Leadership

Domain Key Concepts: Culture, Climate, Vision

Competency 002

The principal knows how to communicate and collaborate with all members of the school community, respond to diverse interests and needs, and mobilize resources to promote student success.

Communication and collaboration are important leadership concepts in every organization. They are particularly important in schools, where having everyone take part in developing, articulating, and implementing plans, ideas, and concepts is essential to innovation and future student success. Competency 002 thus focuses on the role of communication and *collaboration* with *all members of the school community*. As shown in Figure 4.1, it does not say to communicate and collaborate only with the members who you like, who will agree with everything you say, or who are leaders in the school community. It says *all* members. That means we must communicate and collaborate even with people who may not be our favorites, as well as those whose goal in life appears to be to cause trouble at the school. Be nice. Solicit their input. Be objective. What can be identified as useful from the input of each source? Find something of value in every situation. Girl Scouts are taught to always leave a place better than they found it. Should not the same thing be said of educators?

This competency instructs principals to *respond to diverse interests and needs*. Everyone will not have the same interests or needs. Just as there are 31 flavors of ice cream at Baskin-Robbins, there are as many different

Figure 4.1 Competency – Based Principals Are Collaborative

- Collaborating with Families and Other Community Members

- Responding to community interests and needs

- Mobilizing Community Resources

interests and needs in schools as there are people involved. This goes beyond race, gender, and socioeconomics. It delves into specific individual needs that all humans have. Abraham Maslow's (1970) hierarchy of needs goes from lower-level needs of the basics, such as food, clothing, and shelter, to higher-level needs, such as self-confidence, self-awareness, and self-actualization. It may be unrealistic to think we can individualize to the point that all members of the school community will have all their needs met, but the goal of this competency is to try to meet them. Classes do not look the same, act the same, or learn the same way they did in "the good old days." Those days are not coming back—nor should they. Our role is to do everything in our power to respond to the diverse interests and needs of our modern classrooms.

The last component in Competency 002 is *mobilizing resources to promote student success.* This means somebody has to be in charge of getting things together, supplying resources, keeping things organized, and facilitating student success. In this case, that someone is you—the principal. It is your job to mobilize everything necessary to guarantee student growth and productivity. Notice that *mobilize* and *respond* are strong, active verbs. They are not wimpy verbs. They are substantive. The competencies do not use wimpy verbs. We do not need wimpy verbs because we do not need wimpy principals. We need strong, proactive, reflective principals who focus on having a positive school culture and climate that focuses exclusively on the specific vision of the school. Now, let's see some ways that principals can accomplish this goal.

THE PRINCIPAL KNOWS HOW TO . . .

- *Communicate effectively with families and other community members in varied educational contexts.*

The principal must know how to communicate effectively with families and other community members in varied educational contexts. For testing purposes, "varied educational contexts" means everywhere. It also goes deeper than that. In addition to knowing how, the principal must actually do it. There is a big difference between knowing how to do something and actually doing it. There are rude people all over the place who know how to be nice—they simply choose not to be. As a positive, proactive, change-oriented principal, you must know how to communicate professionally and effectively and you must actually do it.

Effectively is the key word here. If families and other community members do not understand what you are saying, writing, or otherwise communicating, then you are not communicating effectively. You may think you are, but if they are not understanding or comprehending what you are saying, you are not getting it done. Be aware of this. It is not other people's job to be better listeners. It is your job to be a better communicator. There may be various reasons why your message is not being understood. The culture and climate of the school may not be aligned with that of the school community. Language or attitudes may be issues. The solution to the communication problem will take analysis and input from families and other community members in "varied educational contexts," that is, everywhere. In other words, you must swallow your pride and go to the source. Talk to the people most closely affected. Solicit input. It is difficult to sell the vision of your school if no one understands what you are saying.

- *Apply skills for building consensus and managing conflict.*

Conflict is an interesting thing. Some people never want any conflict. To have conflict means that people are not agreeing. If people are not agreeing, that means there's diversity of opinion. Hello! Are we not looking for diversity of opinion? If we do not get different views from various people, we'll end up in a muck of status quo–ism, which is exactly where we do not want to be.

Unfortunately, we all know schools that are already there. Worse, they *like* it there and do not want to change.

On the other hand, we definitely do not want people yelling, screaming, pouting, or getting their feelings hurt because they don't feel their opinions are valued or respected. There has to be a middle ground.

That is why applying skills for building consensus and managing conflict are important. There must be divergent opinions to challenge our perceptions and expectations. Divergent opinions challenge our mindsets. This, subsequently, helps us to grow and to see other perspectives. Diverse opinions should be actively solicited, listened to, and shared. After thorough, respectful consideration of multiple suggestions and beliefs, a common ground must be identified. Through skills for building consensus and managing conflict, the principal kneads all of this together, much as a baker kneads dough. If the bread is not kneaded consistently and with great effort over a long period of time, it won't rise. For the school to reach its vision, stakeholders must be taught listening skills, mutual respect, and problem solving. Finally, once a decision is made, everyone must support it. That's part of being a team. Decision making is not an individual effort—it's a group effort and a group consensus. The principal must therefore be skilled in group processes to facilitate agreement from people with different perspectives.

- *Implement effective strategies for systematically communicating with and gathering input from all campus stakeholders.*

To facilitate these group processes and team building, the principal must implement effective strategies for systematically communicating with and gathering input from all campus stakeholders. Notice that it does not say to gather input only from campus stakeholders who will always agree with you. This is another example, as above, where the competencies reach out to divergent opinions from all stakeholders. Remember, the most important three-letter word in the competencies and on the test is *all*. Watch for it in responses. It is an important Sherry. There must be a system for communicating with and gathering input from everyone. This does not happen by chance or good intention. There must be a system. If there is a system, there must be a plan that has been developed. Guess how . . . *collaboratively*. Do everything collaboratively. It is a key to success in learner-centered schools and in passing the TExES exam.

- *Develop and implement strategies for effective internal and external communications.*

Here are two important concepts. Families are important in the education of their children. The first is to develop and implement strategies. By now you may be sick of hearing about all this developing and implementing of virtually everything. Be sick of it later. Right now, take it to heart. You are the facilitator who sees that all this development—Number 1 in the 1–2–3–4 Plan—and implementation occur. In this case, you are facilitating strategies for effective internal and external communication.

This brings us to the second point of effective internal and external communications. There is overlap with the previous discussion of *effective*. If something isn't working, how can it be effective? In using the words *internal* and *external* the competency is trying to make sure you understand that effective communication is not limited to inside the school. You must communicate effectively with all stakeholders, which also includes those external to the school. Families, neighbors, and businesses and churches in the community must understand and support the vision of the school. This cannot occur without strategies for effective internal and external communication. Circulating newsletters, meeting with community groups, visiting places and people outside the school, contacting the media, and using other collaboratively developed strategies to communicate effectively are essential to getting out the message of your vision both inside and outside the school.

Figure 4.2 Families Are Important in the Education of Their Children

- *Develop and implement a comprehensive program of community relations that effectively involves and informs multiple constituencies, including the media.*

Here we go with *develop* and *implement* again. They are Numbers 1 and 3 of the 1–2–3–4 Plan. This time, it is in relation to a comprehensive program of community relations that effectively involves and informs multiple constituencies, including the media. Let's take this one by small increments because there is a lot in it.

First, you develop and implement—collaboratively, of course—your plan of choice. This time, the plan is a comprehensive program of community relations. You do this by involving multiple constituencies from varied contexts. This means you involve many different people from diverse places and backgrounds to help develop the plan. Within this charge is the repetition of *effectively*. It does not do any good to develop a plan, or a comprehensive program, of community relations if it is not effective. If something is not going to work, why do it? Community relations includes, among other things, the way the community will perceive or view the school. Obviously, you want the entire community to view the school well, to support its vision by supporting its curriculum, instructional techniques, programs, and culture. You want the community to be *for* the school, never *against* it. Public sentiment has been known to hang by a thread and to change without warning. That is why it's important that your comprehensive program actually be *comprehensive* by involving lots of people (i.e., multiple constituencies), including the media.

Use the media to your advantage. If your district does not have a public relations specialist who coordinates or speaks for the district, be careful of what you say to the media. Usually, less is best because the media sometimes have an uncanny way of misquoting you, even if you give your statement to them in writing. A savvy and wise city manager once told his staff to be careful about picking a fight with anyone who buys ink by the barrel. Educators, too, must heed this advice. Specifically solicit good working relationships with the media. There could be times when you really need their support. And always be careful of everything you say because it may come back in a printed version that isn't exactly what you had in mind.

- *Provide varied and meaningful opportunities for parents/caregivers to be engaged in the education of their children.*

"Varied and meaningful opportunities" is an important concept. The ideal principal provides an open door and a warm, welcoming climate within and outside of the building. After all, the school belongs to the community, not to its employees. Parents and caregivers, whoever the caregivers may be, deserve to be engaged in the education of their children. Unfortunately, today we have way too many caregivers whom we cannot seem to get involved even when we desperately want their input. This does not mean we can give up. We never give up on anything or anyone. We just keep trying, consistently, day after day, hoping persistence will pay off. You never know what seeds you plant today will reap unknown benefits in the future. So, just keep trying. Never give up.

- *Establish partnerships with parents and caregivers, businesses, and others in the community to strengthen programs and support campus goals.*

Establishing partnerships with virtually everyone is a big deal. If it sounds impossible, remember that we are not dealing with reality. We are dealing with ideal. Collaboration and collegiality on virtually all issues will lead to school improvement. In other words, it will strengthen programs and support campus goals. When we establish partnerships everyone becomes invested in the relationship and its outcomes. That is what we want. We want everyone engaged in strengthening programs and supporting campus goals. We want everyone in a partnership with us, never against us. If there is anyone against us, they are the first with whom we want to work on developing relationships and partnerships. This includes parents and caregivers, businesses, and others—everyone in the school community. Watch for test question responses that address strong collaboration and partnerships with others outside the campus.

- *Communicate and work effectively with diverse groups in the school community to ensure that all students have an equal opportunity for educational success.*

Pay attention to your Sherries here. If they were not important, they would not keep coming up. This time, we are again looking at communicating and working effectively with diverse groups in the school community.

This is critical because even though the concept of working with community members in varied educational contexts and all stakeholders has been brought up repeatedly and both of those include diverse groups, this is such an important issue that they spell it out for you. They do not want you to take any chances of missing the point that *working effectively with diverse groups* is paramount to success. It is a classic example of the teaching strategy of "Tell them. Tell them again with different language. Tell them one more time in still another way. Then, in closing, tell them what they just learned." The competencies want to make sure you know that working effectively with diverse groups is very, very important. Remember that as you lead your school. Remember it while taking the TExES exam and looking at various answers. Look for the answers in which the concept of soliciting input from lots of people of varied backgrounds and experiences is stressed. That's usually the correct answer. Without the total support of diverse groups in the school community, how can you ensure (did you catch that verb?) that all students have an equal opportunity for educational success?

I must elaborate on all students having an equal opportunity for educational success. It is foundationally and constitutionally true in the United States that all people are created equal, but when it comes to education, that's quite a stretch. Every student comes with different experiences and with different baggage. Some arrive at school hungry. Consider Maslow's work. How can anyone concentrate on learning if they're hungry? Hunger is just the tip of the iceberg when it comes to student differences. Can we solve all the social problems of the world? Regretfully, no. We can do everything possible to facilitate every student at our own schools in having, at minimum, an equal opportunity for educational success by attempting to meet their educational and individual needs. Too many of our students do not have anyone who really cares about them. At the ideal school, at least they will have us. If our teachers cannot buy into this philosophy of helping students on all levels, to provide them with an equal opportunity, then guess what? It's time for them to look for a new career.

- *Respond to pertinent political, social, and economic issues in the internal and external environment.*

This concept asks that you keep your eyes open. Be aware of what is going on in the world. Don't let yourself get so caught up in what's going on inside the school that you lose track of what's going on outside the school. This even goes beyond the school community. It involves pertinent political, social, and economic issues around the world. No man is an island, and no school is an island, either. We cannot operate in isolation. Everything going on in the world—and particularly in our communities—has an impact on schools. Be cognizant of local, state, national, and world affairs. Encourage your faculty, staff, and the students to stay up with current events. It is the systems approach to life. Everything is connected. Nothing happens in isolation.

GUESS MY FAVORITE

Have you guessed my favorite? It is the following:

- *Communicate and work effectively with diverse groups in the school community to ensure that all students have an equal opportunity for educational success.*

There's pure poetry in this one—don't miss it. Why are we here if not to ensure that all students have an equal opportunity for educational success? It's what we're all about as educators. If you do not believe in this one, quit now. Education is not for you.

IMPORTANT POINTS TO REMEMBER

- Work and communicate effectively with everyone—both inside and outside the school.
- Encourage discussion and input from people with different opinions while nurturing consensus and managing conflict.
- Community relations can make you or break you. Nurture them!
- Engage parents, caregivers, businesses, and everyone else, including strangers on the street, in partnerships and meaningful opportunities to be a part of the school family.
- Keep your eyes open to respond to everything taking place in the world that could impact students or education.
- Ensure that all students have an equal opportunity for success in every facet of their lives.

Learner-Centered Values and Ethics of Leadership

Domain I: School Community Leadership

Domain Key Concepts: Culture, Climate, Vision

Competency 003

The principal knows how to act with integrity, fairness, and in an ethical and legal manner.

In its simplest form, this competency says the principal should do what is morally right at all times, even if it is not politically correct. This is the classic place to make sure your walk matches your talk. It is one thing to say that all people should be treated with integrity, fairness, and in an ethical and legal manner, but it is something else entirely to practice this ideal. Often, this can be a classic case of "Do as I say, not as I do."

Although all of this may sound easy, we know that it really isn't. The Cadet Prayer at West Point asks God for guidance in doing the "harder right versus the easier wrong." Competency 003 expects educators to do the same thing.

THE PRINCIPAL KNOWS HOW TO . . .

- *Model and promote the highest standard of conduct, ethical principles, and integrity in decision-making, actions, and behaviors.*

Ethics and integrity are displayed in the way you conduct yourself personally and professionally. Actions speak louder than words. Regardless of what kind of lip service is paid to a mantra of all students being able to learn, talk is nothing unless you put what you say into

Figure 5.1   Competency–Based Principals Have a Moral Compass

- Act with integrity.

- Act fairly.

- Act ethically.

- Act legally.

It is one thing to promote the highest standard of conduct, ethical principles, and integrity in decision making, actions, and behaviors. It is an entirely different matter to *model* the same behavior. It's a lot easier said than done, even for those who want to do right. Do not write off this competency as an easy thing to do. It may be the most difficult of all.

- Implement policies and procedures that promote professional educator compliance with the Code. The *Code of Ethics and Standard Practices for Texas Educators* is available for free at **http://info.sos.state.tx.us/pls/pub/ readtac$ext.TacPage?sl=R&app=9&p_dir=&p_rloc=&p_tloc=&p_ ploc=&pg=1&p_tac=&ti=19&pt=7&ch=247&rl=2** (Retrieved November 4, 2012).

practice on a consistent and daily basis. Trust is so easy to destroy, and equally difficult to regain. It is important to listen to your constituents with a truly open mind rather than to make decisions based upon preconceived perceptions. Decisions should be data driven rather than perception driven. It is very hard to repair the damage and credibility among school staff if they think you have made a decision based on bias, partiality, or just plain stubbornness. Constituents need to know and understand why decisions are made. As often as reasonably possible, they should be made collaboratively. People will support what they have helped to develop or decide. Before taking action, ask yourself if it will pass the smell test. If someone else sees you doing something that you think is perfectly fine, would it smell to them? Would it cause suspicion? Would they think you are getting by with doing something they cannot, or should not, do? If so, this action smells. Remember, something can be totally innocent, but given just the right twist, it can appear unethical. Be cautious. Always act with discretion. Err on the side of caution. Someone is always watching and listening and, often, more than likely to repeat what they saw or heard freely . . . and with that dangerous little twist. The concept of modeling and promoting "the highest standard of conduct, ethical principles, and integrity in decision making, actions, and behaviors" may sound like common sense. Unfortunately, too often there is an uncommon lack of common sense. Be careful. Be prudent. As shown in Figure 5.1, always measure everything you do by your moral compass. You have one. Use it.

The *Code of Ethics and Standard Practices for Texas Educators* is basically a common sense document of ethical behaviors. You do not need to memorize it. Review it before the test. Really consider what it says. There is nothing in it that will shock you, but it is a good, solid review for this competency—and for your life as an educator. The test will not ask you to quote it. However, it will expect you to know what it says, to be able to live by it, to model it for others, and to encourage your staff to do likewise. The test will not come directly at you with questions that shout, "Are you ethical?" Rather, your interpretation of ethical behavior will be embedded in the answer choices. Therefore, be on full alert to make sure you select the most ethical response.

- *Apply knowledge of ethical issues affecting education.*

In today's world, the only constant is change. It seems it is becoming a regular occurrence to see or hear that some educator has behaved in an unprofessional, unseemly, or downright illegal manner in relation to a student. This is particularly horrifying in regard to sexual harassment issues for both sexes. Therefore, it is of utmost importance for principals to stay abreast of and be able to apply things learned from current events and legislation in regard to ethical and legal issues involving students, personnel, and the community. You must be the stalwart of ethical behavior in the way you conduct your own life both professionally and personally. Any of these issues could lead to your demise as well as presenting a bad perception for the school. Keep everything you and the system do aboveboard. Do not just assume ethical- and compliance-related issues will take care of themselves. Research what school policies and procedures are in place to ensure they occur. If none exist, make it a priority to see to it that they are developed, articulated, and implemented to ensure the school is in full compliance with the *Code of Ethics and Standard Practices for Texas Educators* as well as all federal, state, and local policies and regulations.

Knowing the ethical thing to do is different from applying it. Make sure you are a model of ethical behavior inside and outside of school. As an administrator, you live life as if in a fishbowl. Like it or not, an entire school and district are watching everything you do.

- *Apply legal guidelines (e.g., in relation to students with disabilities, bilingual education, confidentiality, discrimination) to protect the rights of students and staff members and to improve learning opportunities.*

Two vital responsibilities of any principal are to protect the rights of students and staff members and to improve learning opportunities. It shouldn't be necessary to be reminded of legal guidelines. Individual educational plans (IEPs) provide a good example of the need to apply legal guidelines. If a student with a disability moves to your school and his IEP says he should jump rope backward in the shade of a west-facing tree at 10:01 every morning, you had better make sure he does just that until another admission, review, and/or dismissal meeting (ARD) can be held to modify his care plan. Until then, it is the law.

Various examples of legal guidelines regarding students with disabilities, bilingual education, confidentiality, and discrimination are provided in the competency that addresses concerns within the school community. An easier way to remember which guidelines to apply is to consistently apply them all. If it is the law or a policy, do it. If you truly hate it, contact your legislator or other policymaker to discuss why you hate it and why you think it should be changed.

- *Apply laws, policies, and procedures in a fair and reasonable manner.*

Apply laws, policies, and procedures in a fair and reasonable manner for all people. Do not play favorites. If something could be construed as unethical, immoral, or illegal behavior, don't do it. Do not set yourself up for criticism. Treat rules and people consistently and fairly.

Be consistent. Even if you think there are circumstances where a law, policy, or procedure is cumbersome or irrelevant, as long as it is in place, you must use it. Nothing will get a principal in trouble, inside or outside the school, more than the perception that various people or groups are treated differently from any others. You must be extra careful about this in relation to any family members or friends who are employed by the school. It doesn't take much to give some negative community members something to exaggerate, misrepresent, and spread around. The more a story gets told, the worse it can become. By the time it gets back to you, it could be so distorted you barely even recognize it. Remember, there are people who live by the mantra of "Do not mess up my misperceptions with your facts. I like it in my mixed-up world. I get attention by passing around wrong information. It makes my day." The solution is to proactively avoid giving anyone anything at all to talk about. You do this by applying all laws, policies, and procedures in a fair and reasonable manner and doing so in a manner that is above reproach.

- *Articulate the importance of education in a free democratic society.*

To articulate is to communicate the importance of education to everyone, everywhere. It is the role of all educators, not just administrators, to articulate the importance of education in a free democratic society. If it's not our responsibility, then whose is it? It has been said that today's principals are so busy with trivia and management duties, there's little time left for the role of statesperson that educators traditionally have played. We cannot let this responsibility slip away. It is one we carry with us at school, at home, at church, in the community, and in everything we do.

- *Serve as an advocate for all children.*

There are people who do not understand why special programs—English language literacy, extra- and co-curricular, transportation, and multiple other programs—even need to exist. It is the role of all educators, and particularly principals as role models, to articulate the importance of a free and appropriate education for every child. Some programs, policies, and rules exist due to federal and state legal issues and regulations. Others exist to enhance school programming by school choice. But all programs exist to improve the educational opportunities for every student in the school regardless of whether English is their first language, whether they do not have a stable home life (which, consequently, can cause multiple problems both at school and in society), whether they are involved with drugs, whether they are not totally positive where their next meal is coming from, or whether they appear to simply not understand or care about their own education. The principal must lead the way in stressing the importance of meeting the needs of every student for the short- and long-term benefit of society.

Remember, if advocating for the needs of *all* children is not the responsibility of educators, particularly administrators, then whose responsibility is it? I take this very seriously and want you to do so as well. Our children are our future, our legacy. We cannot write off a single child. To care is not enough; to advocate for children requires action. It means not being afraid to speak up for the oppressed, the downtrodden, the sick, the disabled, or the hungry. It means standing up for those who do not speak English, who have no money, or who struggle with abuse or neglect. It means giving every student a second—or a hundredth—chance to get an education and, to the best of our ability, removing obstacles to their success.

Being an advocate is an emotionally draining experience. You should know that going in. There will be times when you think you just cannot do this anymore. You are tired, frustrated, and just plain spent. When those times occur, take a day or two away from school. Do not feel guilty. You need this time of respite and retreat to recharge physically, emotionally, and spiritually. Take it, and don't look back. Don't answer the phone. Let your soul have the quiet time it needs to rest, reflect, and regain strength away from the business, craziness, and stresses of your life. You will be a better person and a better administrator when you return. If you are going to be an advocate for all children, there are times when you'll feel drained of all energy. But the effort is worth it if you really believe in a free democratic society. The future of that society is our children. They are our future. They are our responsibility.

- *Promote the continuous and appropriate development of all students.*

The key words here are *continuous* and *appropriate.* Students are going to develop regardless. They may or may not develop in appropriate ways. It is the responsibility of the principal, as well as all of society, to see to it that all students have continuous and appropriate development. *Continuous*

Figure 5.2   Ideal Principals Are Advocates for All Children

means all the time, without ceasing. It means you can never give up on seeking to mentor and guide the development of every student with whom you have contact. It is not limited to academic development but to every facet of student maturation. For those who think they did not enter education to take on raising every single child, there is one thing to remember. The role of educators is to nurture every student continuously.

- *Promote awareness of learning differences, multicultural awareness, gender sensitivity, and ethnic appreciation.*

All people, whether they are 3 years old or 50 years old, learn differently. This isn't news, yet for many classrooms in the United States, teachers act as if they don't know this. They continue to stand and deliver instruction that often is not one bit meaningful to the experiences, culture, gender, or ethnicity of students who are held captive in the classroom, sitting there not really listening or caring. And then we wonder about the future of education.

If we know students have different learning styles and modalities, that they come with different experiences, genders, and cultures, why are we treating them as if we thought everyone of them were alike? As positive, proactive, student-centered school leaders, it is imperative that we promote awareness of learning differences, multicultural awareness, gender sensitivity, and ethnic and religious appreciation. Promoting it by articulation only is not enough. You must be in there proactively, role modeling the type of leadership you expect teachers and others to display in classrooms and in the community. Furthermore, you must reward appropriate behavior from your staff members. Praise them. Nurture a vision for the school that includes and appreciates every student, teacher, and community member regardless of their differences.

GUESS MY FAVORITES

It is virtually impossible for me to pick a single favorite in this competency. In fact, I have more favorites in 003 than in all the others, which is saying a lot. Here they are, as if you hadn't guessed:

- *Articulate the importance of education in a free democratic society.*
- *Serve as an advocate for all children.*
- *Promote the continuous and appropriate development of all students.*
- *Promote awareness of learning differences, multicultural awareness, gender sensitivity, and ethnic appreciation.*

IMPORTANT POINTS TO REMEMBER

- Treat every student as if the future of our country depended on how this single human being is nurtured and developed.
- Let your walk match your talk in every facet of your life. This includes your private life as well as your professional life.
- Be ethical, moral, consistent, fair, and legal at all times.
- Students are human beings. They come from different circumstances. Do not try to make them all the same. Do not try to make them into something they are not. Value, cherish, and appreciate their individual cultures, ethnic backgrounds, genders, circumstances, and experiences. Treat every one of them as if they were your own or as if they were the very student who will grow up and marry your child or grandchild. Think about it. Act accordingly.
- One more thing. Be an advocate for all children!

6

Learner-Centered Curriculum Planning and Development

Domain II: Instructional Leadership

Domain Key Concepts: Curriculum, Instruction, Staff Development

Competency 004

The principal knows how to facilitate the design and implementation of curricula and strategic plans that enhance teaching and learning; ensure alignment of curriculum, instruction, resources, and assessment; and promote the use of varied assessments to measure student performance.

Remember that while reviewing Competency 001, we discussed the progression of development, articulation, implementation, and stewardship of the vision of the school? We called it the 1–2–3–4 Plan. The same process is used in Competency 004 as the principal facilitates the design and implementation of curricula and strategic plans that enhance teaching and learning. Notice it says the principal *facilitates* this design. It does not say the principal does it alone.

On the TExES examination, be careful to watch for answers that sound excellent but discuss responsibilities that are not the principal's. The test developers include these to determine whether you are collaborative in your leadership style and whether you delegate and empower others to further their professional growth. An example of this is the principal's facilitating the design and implementation of curricula and strategic plans. By facilitating, the principal supplies needed resources, including time and support, to teachers and others involved in decision making such that appropriate curricula and strategic planning can occur. For example, principals with a secondary teaching background may not feel comfortable teaching in a kindergarten classroom. That's not their job.

But it is their job to ensure that the kindergarten teachers have all the necessary resources, including time and training, to maximize their students' learning. Therefore, principals facilitate the teachers' success. It is not the principals' job to do everything. It is the principals' job to ensure everything gets done.

Strategic planning for curriculum and instruction, as well as for every other school venture, is critically important to teaching and learning. First, identification of campus strengths and weaknesses must occur. This is done by analyzing school and student data. It is followed by systematically analyzing how strengths can be used to support and develop weaknesses. There must be a plan to address every weakness. Without one, you'll simply wander through the wilderness of school administration, hoping student learning will be enhanced somehow. But you'll never be sure it is, because no systematic plan exists to identify goals and strategies for implementation and no assessment tools are in place. As shown in Figure 6.1, exactly how are we assessing programs and curriculum that impact learning? There we are, back to the 1–2–3–4 Plan.

Figure 6.1   The 1–2–3–4 Plan

1. Develop; create.

2. Articulate; communicate.

3. Implement; just do it.

4. Steward; evaluate.

The 1–2–3–4 Plan provides a systematic framework within which every stakeholder in the learning community is working and focused. They should be done in the order presented because each builds on the next. For a campus to be growing, vibrant, and moving toward its goals there must always be a systematic campus improvement plan through which the following tasks are achieved:

- Collaborative identification of campus, grade, or subject goals
- Detailing and implementation of strategies and techniques, including technology use, to attain these goals

- Definition of timelines to be used as benchmarks to measure progress
- Formative and summative assessment to determine if progress has been made
- Continuous modification to enhance the productivity of the plan as measured by increased student learning and progress toward the campus vision

Notice that the key terms of *design* and *implementation* are used repeatedly within the competencies. Watch for those words, or others that mean the same thing, on the test. These are important roles of the principal. They will be embedded in TExES questions and responses.

The competency goes on to focus on the role of the principal to ensure alignment of curriculum, instruction, resources, and assessment. The issue of alignment appears repeatedly in the competencies (see Figure 2.2). It is obviously one of the test designers' favorites. In this case, it relates to curriculum, instruction, resources, and assessment. But what does it mean?

Very simply, it means this: Do these factors—curriculum, instruction, resources, and assessment—work together? A curriculum is *what* is taught. Instruction is *how* it is taught. Resources are the tools used in the instruction of curricula. Assessment, of course, is measurement of the first three factors. Ideally, each of these factors is connected. Appropriate instructional strategies are aligned with what is taught. Appropriate resources to accomplish this goal are budgeted and provided for. Then, the results of these endeavors are tested or alternatively measured. All of this should be documented in the campus plan, lesson plans, and the budget. If any piece is missing, the system will not work efficiently. The result will be a lack of appropriate teaching and learning.

Few educators think they are not testing what is taught at their schools. The only true way to know, however, is through a thorough needs assessment and curriculum alignment. These are major, time-consuming projects if they are done right. And if they are not done right, they are not worth doing at all. That means they are not something you can accomplish at Tuesday afternoon's faculty meeting. It will take longer than that just to figure out what needs to be done and how to do it. Needs assessments and curriculum alignments should be well thought out and systematically planned with significant input from the entire learning community. All these data go into the development and refinement of campus goals and progress toward the campus vision.

Sometimes surprising things are revealed. Although teachers may think they are spending significant amounts of time teaching a specific concept, the curriculum alignment could reveal that they aren't. It should come as no surprise when analysis of test data reveals student weaknesses in the same area. The same can be true conversely. Sometimes too much time is spent on a concept students have mastered, and it's time to move on.

Needs assessments and curricula alignments should occur at the district as well as the campus level. Data analysis is exceedingly important. It is the foundation on which sound curricular and instructional decisions can

Figure 6.2 How Are We Measuring Student Learning to Ensure Educational Accountability?

be made. It allows us to ensure, not simply to hope, that our schools will improve. Ensuring, not hoping, is what our quest toward the campus vision demands. Anything less is a waste of time.

The ideal principal promotes the use of varied assessments to measure student performance. That means that, contrary to popular belief, the Texas Assessment of Academic Skills is not the be all and end all of student assessment. It is one tool, although a very important one in Texas, by which we assess our students. But there are many other, alternative forms of assessment available that should also be used. Successful schools often use a constructivist approach to teaching. Authentic assessment through student demonstrations of learning as well as performance and project development are also used. We must capitalize on the use of multiple intelligences, multisensory, and other forms of assessment that address individual learning styles. Are standardized forms of assessment important? Of course. But there are also many students, including adult learners, who for various reasons simply do not do well on standardized or other forms of paper-and-pencil tests. This doesn't mean they aren't intelligent or that they aren't learning. It means their learning must be measured by varied assessments. In the ideal school, led by the ideal principal, varied assessments are used to measure student performance.

THE PRINCIPAL KNOWS HOW TO . . .

- *Facilitate effective campus curriculum planning based on knowledge of various factors (e.g., emerging issues, occupational and economic trends, demographic data, student learning data, motivation theory, teaching and learning theory, principles of curriculum design, human developmental processes, and legal requirements).*

The principal is the instructional leader of the school. To be the instructional leader, the principal must facilitate campus curriculum planning based on knowledge of various factors. These factors include, but are not limited to, emerging issues, occupational and economic trends, demographic data, student learning data, motivation theory, teaching and learning theory, principles of curriculum design, human developmental processes, and legal requirements. By analyzing these various factors, you are using triangulation, as discussed in Chapter 3; that is, you will facilitate curriculum planning and implementation. You do not have to be an expert on every issue. You will empower others as you collaboratively integrate curricular planning for school improvement.

- *Facilitate the use of sound, research-based practice in the development, implementation, and evaluation of campus curricular, co-curricular, and extracurricular programs.*

We've returned to the 1–2–3–4 Plan of development, articulation, implementation, and stewardship/evaluation theme. You can see how this progression of steps is used over and over again in the competencies. This time, it is in reference to the use of sound, research-based practice . . . of campus curricular, co-curricular, and extracurricular programs. You could substitute the word *all* for the words *curricular, co-curricular,* and *extracurricular* programs. The idea is that sound, research-based practice is developed, implemented, and evaluated.

Your own ongoing professional development is important. Just because you complete your preparation program and certification requirements does not mean that you can stop learning. You must continue to read, study, attend professional conferences, participate in discussions, and conduct action research to stay current. Do not make the mistake of planning professional development activities for your staff and none for yourself. You also need—and deserve—to grow. Your campus staff needs to see that you value development enough to participate in growth activities and not just tell them to do it. They will see you walk the walk, and this will stimulate their professional growth. Your collective growth will have positive benefits to teaching and learning at your school.

- *Facilitate campus participation in collaborative district planning, implementation, monitoring, and revision of curriculum to ensure appropriate scope, sequence, content, and alignment.*

By now you are recognizing the common pattern of planning (or developing), implementing, monitoring, and revising (or modifying) of virtually everything. This time, it is in reference to curriculum, ensuring (did you catch *ensure?*) appropriate scope, sequence, content, and alignment.

Alignment, by now, is our good friend. We know what that means. It means to match up everything appropriately to make sure it is doing what it is supposed to do. Scope and sequence are the big and little pictures of curriculum planning. Scope is where you are going. Sequence is the path to get you there. Think of it as a Covey (1990) "begin-with-the-end-in-mind" concept with the scope of the curriculum content the end you have in mind.

Bringing all this together, the principal is the facilitator of campus participation in collaborative (sound familiar?) district planning. Notice that this time the principal is working with the district in addition to the campus itself for district planning, implementation, monitoring, and revision of curriculum. Last, the principal is ensuring that appropriate (not just what comes next in the textbook) scope, sequence, content, and alignment occur. This is a very heavy responsibility.

- *Facilitate the use of appropriate assessments to measure student learning and ensure educational accountability.*

Appropriate is another word to watch for. It comes up over and over. This time, it is in relation to assessment. There are all kinds of assessments. Different ones may have different values for different situations. No specific form of assessment is perfect for every student or situation. Different topics as well as different student learning styles and modalities require different forms of assessment. That is the point the test designers try to make with the phrase *appropriate assessments to measure student learning and ensure* (ensure, again) *educational accountability.* The assessment must be appropriate, or there will not be true accountability. Think of it as a validity and reliability comparison. If the assessment is not appropriate, there can be no true educational accountability.

- *Facilitate the use of technology, telecommunications, and information systems to enrich the campus curriculum.*

Domain III discusses technology and information systems in relation to the management of the school. In this component, technology, telecommunications, and information systems are tools to be used to enrich the campus curriculum. Domain II focuses on curriculum, instruction, and staff development, so the technology issues here are curriculum and instruction related. It is the role of the principal to facilitate the use of all forms of technology within the curriculum appropriately.

- *Facilitate the effective coordination of campus curricular, co-curricular, and extracurricular programs in relation to other district programs.*

The principal is the person responsible for tying all the different programs and facets of the school together, making sure they are aligned and not in conflict, and ensuring that everything runs properly and in congruence with the campus vision. As such, you must facilitate the effective coordination of campus curricular, co-curricular, and extracurricular programs in relation to other district programs. Notice that it does not say you have to do all this single-handedly, and you won't unless your goal is sheer exhaustion. You are to facilitate these programs and activities not just in relation to your campus but in relation to other district programs as well. As facilitator and coordinator, you are the liaison for making sure all these things run smoothly and in conjunction with campus goals and priorities.

- *Promote the use of creative thinking, critical thinking, and problem solving by staff members and other campus stakeholders involved in curriculum design and delivery.*

This is an important point. It is directed toward the heart of curricular and instructional issues. The principal must promote the use of creative thinking, critical thinking, and problem solving. Is that not the purpose of education? Should not all curriculum and instructional techniques be geared toward the development of *creative thinking, critical thinking, and problem solving* from students and from the entire learning community? This should be one of our most primary goals and a definite focus of our campus vision. If it is not, we have missed a significant purpose in our existence.

It goes on to say that campus stakeholders involved in curriculum design and delivery should participate in this creative and critical thinking and problem solving. Is that not what we just said? Are we not brilliant? Next time *we* can develop TExES. What do you think? We could exercise some creative and critical thinking to problem solve the situation.

GUESS MY FAVORITE

I know this is going to come as a big surprise, but my favorite is:

- *Promote the use of creative thinking, critical thinking, and problem solving by staff and other campus stakeholders involved in curriculum design and delivery.*

IMPORTANT POINTS TO REMEMBER

- Facilitate everything. Dictate nothing.
- Triangulate everything by looking at various forms of data to make informed decisions.
- Empower others but ensure things happen that are supposed to happen.
- Ensure that curriculum, instruction, technology, and assessment are appropriate.
- Make sure all campus and district programs are coordinated appropriately.
- Promote, stress, facilitate, and ensure that everyone involved in the school community is using creative and critical thinking to facilitate problem solving in all areas.

Learner-Centered Instructional Leadership and Management

Domain II: Instructional Leadership

Domain Key Concepts: Curriculum, Instruction, Staff Development

Competency 005

The principal knows how to advocate, nurture, and sustain an instructional program and a campus culture that are conducive to student learning and staff professional growth.

Remember while reviewing Competency 001 that we discussed facilitating the development, articulation, implementation, and stewardship of a vision, that is, the 1–2–3–4 Plan? Competency 005 is its sister. This time, instead of focusing on the vision of the school, we focus on the instructional program and campus culture, but the idea is the same. Both times the principal must advocate, nurture, and sustain something, whether that something is the campus vision or culture for the instructional programs or the application of best practices for the development of a comprehensive professional growth plan.

It is obvious that the principal should advocate virtually anything that is conducive to student learning and staff professional development, but that isn't enough. What if there are principals whose walk does not match their talk? I know that's an amazing concept, but believe it or not, there are some out there. It will not be you. You will go beyond advocating, to nurturing. What is nurturing? Think of parenting. Think of how parents look after, feed, protect, and do everything within their capabilities to make sure their children have everything they need to

Figure 7.1 Competency–Based Principals Provide Leadership

- Promote a positive school culture.

- Provide an effective instructional program.

- Apply best practices for student learning.

- Design comprehensive professional growth plans.

thrive. Now think of the instructional programs and campus climate as your children. You cannot just leave the school community with a curriculum guide and hope for the best. You have to nourish and protect it, and sometimes you have to wipe away the tears. It's your responsibility to comfort, discipline, and nurture the members of your community because you want them to grow up to be wonderful human beings. You do it because you love them.

The same is true in nurturing your campus. You must nourish, cuddle, and comfort everyone involved in your school community. This includes students, teachers, staff members, and families. You must be the iron hand with the velvet glove when you discipline them. You must wipe their tears when they fall down, and you must celebrate their joys and triumphs. This is how you develop a family. Your school is a family. For too many children, the school may be the closest thing to a family they have. They may act as if they don't care what goes on, but deep inside they do. Teachers and other staff members do, too. You are the shepherd of the flock. Take care of it. That's what nurturing the entire campus means, and it includes student learning and staff professional growth. Encourage staff members in their pursuits toward improving student learning as they seek to enhance their own professional growth. Reward their efforts and celebrate their successes. Your campus is growing up around you. You are the parent. You are nurturing your children. You are feeding your flock. The real rewards are intrinsic as you see increased student and staff learning.

So you have advocated and nurtured this learning climate, but how do you sustain it? This is similar to stewardship of the vision that we discussed in Competency 001. In fact, advocating, nurturing, and sustaining are good ways to be a good steward. It is really difficult to sustain something, because once basic goals have been met, there is a basic human tendency to lessen the intensity of effort. And when intensity lessens, so does our passion and then our commitment to a cause greater than us. We cannot allow our own passion, or that of anyone else, to lessen. We must always keep our focus on the vision of the school. If we simply maintain and do not advance, we become the status quo we have worked so hard to change. If we accept the status quo, we soon become stagnant. Anything stagnant soon begins to stink. Who could possibly want a stinking school or principal?

Not us. We want a growing, vibrant, intense, warm, supportive campus. That is why it is imperative that you sustain the focus on current, research-based curriculum, instruction, assessment, and growth for students and staff. Keeping this sustenance constant can be physically, emotionally, and spiritually draining on everyone, including you. Sometimes you have to step back, retreat, and reflect. You have to regroup. Sometimes you may need to take a day off to stay home and let your soul take precedence over your body and mind. The difference between hope and despair is often nothing more than a good night's sleep. It is amazing what rest can do. You need it to meet students' sociological, linguistic, and legal needs.

The same is true for your staff. They work hard, too. There will be times when they need a few minutes or even a day to rest, to regroup, and to get their acts together again. There's no crime in this for you or for them. Does it cost to pay a substitute for a day? Yes, it does. Some schools say they cannot afford it. But the cost of a substitute could be an investment that is well worth it if a teacher comes back refreshed and refocused on helping students become all they can be. The ideal principal works creatively to allow time for staff members to reflect, refocus, and learn. This constitutes a learning community.

Figure 7.2   Principals as Contemporary Cultural Anthropologists

Competency–based principals serve as sociologists, linguists, legal experts, and contemporary cultural anthropologists by

- Understanding contexts,

- Responding to contexts, and

- Influencing contexts.

THE PRINCIPAL KNOWS HOW TO . . .

- *Facilitate the development of a campus learning organization that supports instructional improvement and change through ongoing study of relevant research and best practice.*

The principal is the learning leader of the campus. Effective principals participate in many different types of professional growth and development to study relevant research and best practice. They are current and knowledgeable about new strategies and techniques. They share their knowledge with the rest of the school and community, always striving to infuse new ideas on their campuses. They are lifelong learners in the truest sense of the word. They are not reading, researching, attending conferences, visiting other campuses, or participating in discussions with other professionals just because they should. They are doing it because their hearts are in it. They love learning and want to share that love with others. In this case, the others are members of the school community. Because of this nurturance of adult learning, they are continuously trying new ideas that support instructional improvement and change. The idea is never to quit trying to improve, never to quit asking how we can do things better, and never, ever to settle for the status quo.

- *Facilitate the implementation of sound, research-based instructional strategies, decisions, and programs in which multiple opportunities to learn and be successful are available to all students.*

We continue here as you, a wonderful, change-oriented principal, facilitate the implementation of sound, research-based instructional strategies, decisions, and programs. But you don't stop there. You don't want to take any chances of status quo–ism setting in. You are constantly leading the campus to question new ways to help every student, motivated or not, to learn. You sustain a continuous emphasis on quality as defined by students learning and learning well. To do that, campus strategies, decisions, and programs must provide multiple opportunities, not just one or two opportunities, for all students to be successful. Notice it doesn't say that just the students who are motivated or are class officers will be successful. It says *all* students. That means everyone.

- *Create conditions that encourage staff members, students, families or other caregivers, and the community to strive to achieve the campus vision.*

Creating conditions in the learning environment is part of developing a nurturing and supportive campus climate. Long-term effectiveness and productivity are dependent on a good working and learning environment. Encouraging others in positive ways to think outside of the box, to take risks, and to respond to and appreciate diversity of backgrounds and experiences are all examples of nurturing the campus vision. All stakeholders, including staff members, students, families or other caregivers, and the

Figure 7.3 Everyone Is Necessary to Achieve a Student-Focused Campus Vision

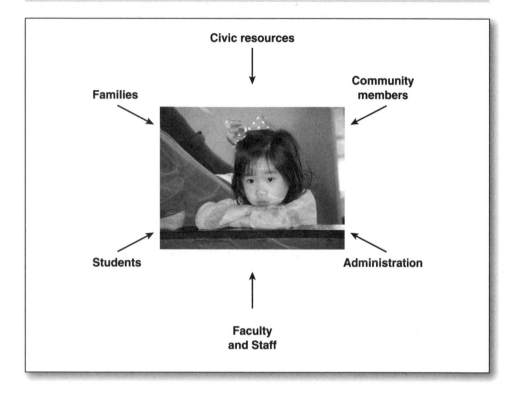

community, must be encouraged and nurtured to work hard, to strive to achieve the campus vision. The campus vision always entails excellence. Excellence is not achieved without taking risks, trying new strategies and programs, implementing new research and best practices; it is not achieved without shared decision making. Together we build. Together we succeed.

- *Ensure that all students are provided high-quality, flexible instructional programs with appropriate resources and services to meet individual student needs.*

Notice that the verb used is *ensure*. Ensure is a strong verb that means to guarantee, not to hope, that success will occur. As a truly great principal, one that passes the TExES exam right off the bat, you will ensure, not hope, that every student in your school is provided high-quality, flexible instructional programs. You will be certain your budget is aligned with your campus goals such that appropriate resources and services are available to achieve the vision. Your campus will never settle for the same old ordinary routine of daily practice. Your campus will constantly be trying new things, infusing new programs, experimenting with different techniques, conducting action research, and being vibrant and alive with creative possibilities to meet individual student needs.

There will be teachers and others who do not want to become actively engaged in any part of students' lives except the cognitive aspects. They will feel that it isn't their job or their business to attempt to meet individual student needs. They are wrong. It is part of our role as professional educators to act with integrity and fairness and in an ethical and legal manner as described in Competency 003. Of course, it is more demanding physically and emotionally to attempt to actively engage in meeting individual student needs. These needs go beyond basic academics. There are other facets to students' lives. Nonetheless, there is a fine line between being interested and supportive and being intrusive. Good principals walk that fine line and encourage their staff to walk along with them to support the needs of all students.

- *Use formative and summative student assessment data to develop, support, and improve campus instructional strategies and goals.*

Here is a simple way to keep the terms *formative* and *summative* straight in your mind. The first four letters of formative are "form." When you form something, you take part in its creation from the beginning. Therefore, formative assessment comes at the beginning, or near the beginning, of planning instruction, programs, needs assessments, community endeavors, and so forth.

On the other hand, the first letters of summative are "sum," as in "summarize." In adding, the sum is the total of the numbers. It is what you get when you are finished and add up everything. The same is true of summative assessment. Summative assessment, similar to summative staff evaluative conferences, comes at the end when you are summarizing a situation. Therefore, by using various data sources for both formative and summative assessment, the campus team can get a better, more global picture of how students are growing, learning, and developing. That is our goal. We want to use many different sources of data, taken at different points to develop, support, and improve campus instructional strategies and goals. If we do not use both formative and summative information, then intelligent, nonbiased, data-driven decision making cannot occur. Without that, why should anyone be surprised when measurable progress toward campus goals is not made? If we do not know where we are, how can we know where we're going and whether we're making progress on the journey? What gets measured gets done. Without continuous formative and summative assessment, progress is only optional. Lack of measurable progress is not an option. We want every child to grow, learn, and succeed. We also want every teacher, paraprofessional, and staff member to grow, learn, and succeed. Therefore, we set goals, we determine how we are going to meet them, and then we use both formative and summative student data to improve everything we do.

- *Facilitate the use and integration of technology, telecommunications, and information systems to enhance learning.*

We are in the fifth of nine competencies. This is the first direct reference to technology. That doesn't mean that technology hasn't been important in other facets of the school, particularly in the development of vision, goals, and instructional strategies. This is why its use must be integrated into all parts of planning, curriculum, instruction, programs, and into the facilities themselves. Ever-changing and expanding technology is here to stay. As principal, you will facilitate the use and integration of technology, telecommunications, and information systems to enhance learning. You will use team collaborative planning as well as formative and summative assessment to determine how this will occur. Information systems will be up-to-date to facilitate the efficient management of data. Telecommunications will be innovative and student centered. Partnerships with businesses, regional service centers, other schools, and universities will be enhanced through networking. As principal, you will facilitate new and innovative ways to integrate the use of technology to enhance learning for everyone, including yourself.

- *Facilitate the implementation of sound, research-based theories and techniques of teaching, learning, classroom management, student discipline, and school safety to ensure a campus environment conducive to teaching and learning.*

An easy way to address this is to put a parenthesis before the word *teaching* and another parenthesis after *safety.* We could then substitute the word *everything* for *teaching, learning, classroom management, student discipline, and school safety.* Of course, it is the responsibility of the principal to facilitate the implementation of sound, research-based theories

Figure 7.4 Integrated Technology and Vision Alignment

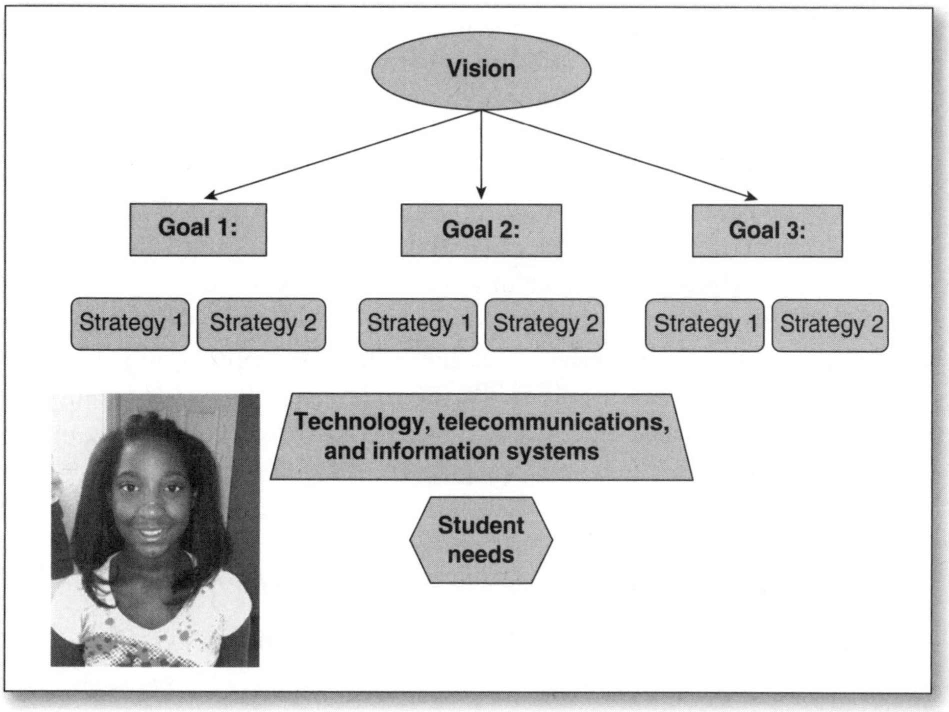

and techniques of everything. What are we supposed to do? Use sound, research-based theories for some things and not others? What can we exclude? Nothing. Therefore, you can consider teaching, learning, classroom management, student discipline, and school safety an elaboration of the word *everything*. The writers of the competencies wanted to elaborate on specific, sound, research-based theories and techniques with examples. All of these—and everything else that takes place in the entire school community—should exist for the single purpose of ensuring a campus environment that is conducive to teaching and learning. This is why we're here. It's our job and our place in society. It's what we do. We use sound, research-based theories and techniques as our tools to enhance teaching and learning and to create a better world.

- *Facilitate the development, implementation, evaluation, and refinement of student services and activity programs to fulfill academic, developmental, social, and cultural needs.*

We have seen this process before. In fact, by now we're old friends with facilitating the development, implementation, evaluation, and refinement of virtually everything, that is, the 1–2–3–4 Plan. We have used it with shared vision, curriculum, instruction, assessment, and staff development. Now we are applying the same process to student services and activity programs.

There are some who erroneously think student services and activity programs, such as climate and culture, are unimportant. They think these are frills and not necessary to student learning. They are wrong. Student services and activity programs help constitute campus climate and culture. They help define who we are, what we value, what we appreciate, what our traditions are, and the subtle nuances that make one school different from another. They are the things that make us unique. We should not try to be any other school. We should seek to develop, nurture, and capitalize on the special things that fulfill the academic, developmental, social, and cultural needs of our school's students and community.

Each school will have its own student services and activity programs. There will be some commonalities among most schools such as football, volleyball, band, and art. But there will be different programs that are successful at one school and less so at another. There is nothing wrong with that. What's important is that each school has the appropriate programs to meet the needs of their students academically, developmentally, socially, and culturally. Work collaboratively with your students, faculty, staff, and community to find new and innovative ways to involve and engage as many people as possible in services and programs that enhance the vision of the school and community.

- *Analyze instructional needs and allocate resources effectively and equitably.*

When I ran for my first term on our school board, my campaign treasurer went around telling people, "Show me the money!" He knew support without financial contributions was great, but it wouldn't help us fund the campaign. Running any campaign is expensive. I was fortunate to have many friends and supporters to help study and define the issues and community as well as to help solicit the necessary resources. Without the nickels and dimes and grassroots support of citizens from a diversity of backgrounds, I would not have had the financial support necessary to fund my campaign. Thank goodness it paid off!

The same is true inside our schools. We have to study and analyze the instructional needs of students. We know that to make intelligent, informed, nonbiased decisions, we must use many types of data. Therefore, our analysis becomes an issue of, "Show me the data." Without appropriate data, we cannot pinpoint specific instructional needs and allocate resources effectively and equitably.

This is another example of the issue of alignment. The campus vision must be collaboratively developed and articulated. Specific goals that meet instructional needs of students must be determined. All the resources necessary to meet these campus goals must then be included in the school's budget. Conversely, there should be nothing in the budget that is not reflected in the campus goals. When the campus goals and budget match, they are aligned. When something appears in one but not the other, they are not aligned. As we've discussed, the same is true of other aspects of campus administration: Curriculum and assessment must be aligned, as must campus and individual needs and staff professional development. For a campus to be effective, everything must be perfectly aligned (Figure 7.5).

Figure 7.5 For a Campus to Be Effective, Everything Must Be Perfectly Aligned

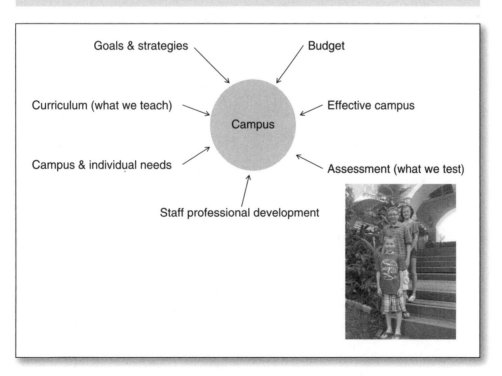

- *Analyze the implications of various factors (e.g., staffing patterns, class scheduling formats, school organizational structures, student discipline practices) for teaching and learning.*

This is similar to the last time we saw a list of examples. Inside the parentheses, you could substitute the word *everything* again. As part of the advocacy, nurturance, and sustenance of proactive student learning, the principal studies data from myriad sources. Through a collaborative and shared decision-making process, the team analyzes the implications of various factors that affect teaching and learning. These include, but are not limited to, staffing patterns, class scheduling formats, school organizational structures, and student discipline practices. Nothing is left out or exempt. The campus team is continuously observant of changes in the learning environment, ready to respond proactively to potential problems by solving them before they develop. There is nothing worse than to play the "if only" game. "If only we had done this," or "if only we had done that, such and such would not have occurred and created this big mess!" By analyzing the contextual implications of various factors (societal, familial, socioeconomic, linguistic, etc.) of teaching and learning, informed, intelligent, and proactive (vs. *reactive*) decision making can occur.

- *Ensure responsiveness to diverse sociological, linguistic, cultural, and other factors that may affect students' development and learning.*

This is a great one. It begins with the strong verb *ensure*. It does not say encourage, solicit, or hope. It says you will ensure responsiveness to diverse sociological, linguistic, cultural, and other factors. That means you must see to it that the school community is responsive to the needs of its students. There are no excuses. The diversity of sociological, linguistic, cultural, and other factors will be addressed. They will not be left to chance or whim. All students and community members will be valued and appreciated for their uniqueness. We will be proactive in our responsiveness to any factor that

Figure 7.6   Diverse Sociological, Linguistic, and Cultural Factors Impact Learning

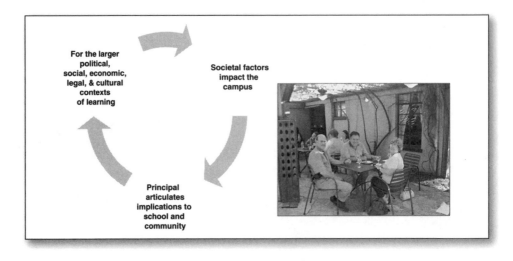

may affect—not that *will* affect—students' development and learning. We leave nothing to chance.

Competency 003 supports the same concept in relation to integrity, fairness, and ethics because the principal promotes awareness of learning differences, multicultural awareness, gender sensitivity, and ethnic appreciation. All of these are diversity factors. The point is basic: The development and learning of every student is paramount. We are here for each of them, regardless of whom they are or whether they have 16 tattoos or green hair. Ensuring responsiveness to diversity that may affect students' development and learning shall be addressed because the principal is ensuring that it will be.

This is indeed an ethics issue. Educators who do not have strong convictions about responding to anything that affects students' development and learning should look for a new career.

GUESS MY FAVORITES

I have two particular favorites in this competency.

- *Facilitate the implementation of sound, research-based instructional strategies, decisions, and programs in which multiple opportunities to learn and be successful are available to all students.*
- *Ensure responsiveness to diverse sociological, linguistic, cultural, and other factors that may affect students' development and learning.*

IMPORTANT POINTS TO REMEMBER

- The principal is the shepherd of the school, advocating, nurturing, and sustaining everything that affects student learning and staff professional growth.
- All students, regardless of any factor, must have multiple research-based opportunities to learn and be successful.
- It is important to create conditions that nurture and sustain a supportive campus climate and culture focused on student learning and staff professional development.
- Formative and summative assessment data must be used from many different sources to facilitate informed decision making.
- Campus goals must be aligned with the budget and vice versa. The same is true for curriculum with assessment and campus needs with staff development.
- Technology should be integrated everywhere.
- Student activities and programs directly affect academic, developmental, social, and cultural needs and are an important part of the campus culture and climate.
- Respond appropriately to anything with the potential to affect students in any way.
- Sustain the stewardship of student and staff success.

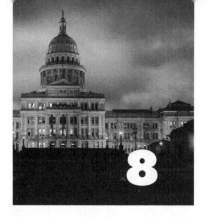

Human Resources Leadership and Management

Domain II: Instructional Leadership

Domain Key Concepts: Curriculum, Instruction, Staff Development

Competency 006

The principal knows how to implement a staff evaluation and development system to improve the performance of all staff members, select and implement appropriate models for supervision and staff development, and apply the legal requirements for personnel management.

Principals are evaluators of all staff on their campuses. Although others may also evaluate some employees such as maintenance and custodial workers, the principal is still primarily responsible for staff evaluation. Most, but not all, Texas school districts participate in the Professional Development Assessment System (PDAS) for the evaluation of teachers. Districts may use an alternative assessment system provided it meets state guidelines. Regardless, teachers are evaluated through a consistent district assessment system. Administrators must be trained and certified in the district model before they can assess teachers. Likewise, all other staff members fall into various district-selected evaluation processes. The responsibility therefore lies with the principal to implement a staff evaluation and development system. The purpose of staff evaluation and development systems is to improve the performance of all staff members.

Although all principals participate in staff evaluation, they do not always follow through with the second piece of this directive: development. Although everyone is willing to give lip service to staff development, in the business of leading and managing a school, staff development is often neglected. How can we nurture and sustain growth for students if we do not make a conscientious effort to plan for the nurturance and growth of staff? This may not make sense, but it happens. It's usually not intentional but more a case of the "squeaky wheel getting the oil." Other things appear to be more pressing, more immediate, and more tangible.

Regardless, this is wrong. We must feed the flock. How can we expect teachers to nurture and sustain students if we do not nurture and sustain teachers? This is done through a systematic plan for staff development. It doesn't consist of putting listings of regional service center course offerings in their boxes and hoping they will attend. Professional development activities for all staff members must be planned and included in the campus budget. Individual and campus needs assessments, personal assessments, disaggregation of testing and other campus data, community input, and other factors must be analyzed, discussed, planned, budgeted, implemented, and evaluated. As always, each component of individual and total staff development should be followed by the question, "How can we do it better?" This key question is a starting point for reflection, analysis, and action research on any topic.

When we finish something, say, an annual project, it's easy to consider our responsibility over for the time being. This is wrong—we're only half way there. Unless we ask ourselves how we can do it better next time, we'll keep doing what we've always done. And if we keep doing what we've always done, we'll keep getting what we've always gotten. We can—and must—do better. Staff development at the personal and campus level is the starting point for curricular, instructional, campus, and personal growth. It's a necessity to stop a potentially great school from becoming just another status quo campus. We want positive, proactive campuses ready to lead the charge for a better society. If we are not proactively planning for individual and campus development, our actions say we are content with what we have. Are you? If not, implement a staff evaluation and development system to improve the performance of all staff members.

As a part of this process, principals must select and implement appropriate models for supervision and staff development. Regardless of the evaluation system in place for teachers and other staff members, principals must make sure they are using an appropriate model. This will be determined by individual campus needs as well as by district policy. Nonetheless, two things are always required: visibility and communication. Principals cannot isolate themselves in their offices. They must proactively make the time to be visible in classrooms, halls, gymnasiums, the cafeteria, and everywhere else. The "MBWA model" (management by wandering around) has great merit. Staff and students need to see you on a regular basis, outside your office, actively involved on campus and in the community. They must see you "walk the walk" of professional development by seeking to develop yourself. Not only should you seek to learn, you should actively communicate and share what you've learned. Communication is a strong key in keeping every channel of opportunity and dialogue open. Open, consistent communication can avert or ease most problems, and routine visibility facilitates this communication.

Development opportunities are not limited to attending conferences or workshops. Reading good books and literature, keeping abreast of current research and best practices, inviting guest speakers to the school, or visiting other campuses to see how they address similar issues are examples of professional development. Always follow up development activities with frank, open discussion. Remember, communication is everything. We learn from each other. We grow together. We share insights. Sometimes we agree, and sometimes we don't. The campus benefits from collective discussion and collaboration on current issues and trends, but without a systematic, planned effort toward growth and development, we don't have enough information for discussion.

Principals must be prepared to face the less positive aspects of management as well. Staff observations, walk-throughs, and documentation are essential to leadership, but they also must be legal. Principals must know and apply the legal requirements for personnel management. You may want to fire an employee on the spot, but unless he or she has done something outside significant policy or legal guidelines, you simply cannot. You must document and provide due process. You must follow established campus and district policy. You must follow the chain of command. Make it your business to know district policy and legal parameters. You do not want to guess at a critical moment.

Furthermore, as a part of staff development, be sure your entire faculty and staff members are cognizant of any legal or policy changes that take place. Ignorance of the law is not an acceptable excuse. It can also get you into a lot of trouble. It's difficult to improve the world one school at a time when you've been fired for making a stupid mistake. Make sure you apply the legal requirements for personnel management and every other aspect of school leadership.

THE PRINCIPAL KNOWS HOW TO . . .

- *Work collaboratively with other campus personnel to develop, implement, evaluate, and revise a comprehensive campus professional development plan that addresses staff needs and aligns professional development with identified goals.*

Part of the vision of the school must include the professional development of all staff members. If we as professionals are not growing and developing, we are standing still. If we are standing still, we become stagnant. Therefore, it is imperative that the development of all staff members, including yourself, be considered, planned for, implemented, evaluated, and funded.

The first step is a needs assessment to determine the actual versus perceived needs and interests of the staff. Once these are identified, collaborate with other campus personnel to develop, implement, evaluate, and revise a comprehensive campus professional development plan.

This four-step model, the 1–2–3–4 Plan—modified here to develop, implement, evaluate, and revise—is evident in various forms throughout the competencies. First, we develop the plan. Next, we implement it. It accomplishes nothing to have a plan on paper or to present it to the school board but never to put it into action. Next, we evaluate it. Nothing is perfect—anything worth doing is worth evaluating. It is through evaluation, assessment, and measurement that we determine the value of the program, plan, model, curriculum, or teaching strategy we're implementing. Once we know a project's strengths and weaknesses, we finish the process by completing the necessary revisions to make it more efficient, timely, and productive. Staff development, as with everything else that occurs in our schools, must be directly linked to campus-identified goals. The evaluation process is one tool to ensure we are making measurable progress toward their attainment. Figure 8.1 illustrates the flow of campus needs, viewed as the foundation on which staff development is built. Staff development should directly connect to campus goals and vision attainment.

- *Facilitate the application of adult learning principles and motivation theory to allow campus professional development activities, including the use of appropriate content, processes, and contexts.*

Faculty and other staff members are adult learners and must be treated as such. They have their own unique set of motivations and inhibitors. Principals and central office administrators who work on staff development activities must base them on adult learning principles and motivation theory. In addition, keep in mind that adults appreciate having food and drinks at after-school meetings. They are tired and usually ready to go home. Attending after-school meetings is usually not at the top of their "Fun Things to Do in the Afternoon" list. Snacks show appreciation and

Figure 8.1 The Campus Success Flowchart

Campus needs ⟶ Staff development ⟶ Goals ⟶ Vision

give them energy to keep going through the afternoon meeting. Busy adults also appreciate well-planned meetings that do not require them to stay for hours at a time. In-depth discussions, brainstorming, and problem solving should be scheduled for other times. All staff development programs should include the use of appropriate content, processes, and contexts. It should be relevant and meaningful. It should have purpose. It should be on their level. Most of all, it should be interesting and relate to personal and campus goals. Anything less is a waste of valuable time that none of us has to spare.

- *Allocate appropriate time, funding, and other needed resources to ensure the effective implementation of professional development plans.*

Time is a common denominator for virtually everything that takes place in school. It is also one of the first things to be neglected in planning. Without time to study, discuss, and plan, it doesn't matter if a school is the richest in the state or if teachers have every conceivable curriculum and resource at their fingertips. Teachers must have time to pilot and evaluate the curriculum in their classrooms. Time supersedes everything. Watch for TExES answers that capitalize on this concept. Time management is critical. Good principals know and help teachers "get out of the box" by planning creative ways to use their time. Principals must then allocate appropriate time, funding, and other needed resources to ensure (remember *ensure?*) the effective implementation of professional development plans.

Although funding, budgeting, and resource management are addressed specifically in Domain III, it is important to connect them to staff development in Domain II. Similar to time procurement and management, we won't get very far without appropriate funding and other needed resources. There have been quite a few lawsuits addressing school finance equity to prove that point. Although progress on the state level has been made, the issue is far from settled. In the meantime, principals must ensure that all resources are aligned with the campus vision and goals. This includes time for planning, study, observations, conferencing, and so forth. Every resource included in the budget must be aligned with at least one campus goal. The reverse is also true. All resources necessary to implement strategies, programs, and so forth toward campus goal attainment must be identified and included in the budget (revisit Figures 3.1–3.6). Without both pieces of this equation, appropriate resources will not be forthcoming and available. In the end, students will not have appropriate resources for learning, and staff members will not have the appropriate resources for growth and development. The budget must be aligned with campus goals, and resources must be used and managed appropriately.

- *Implement effective, appropriate, and legal strategies for the recruitment, screening, selection, assignment, induction, development, evaluation, promotion, discipline, and dismissal of campus staff.*

We have already discussed the importance of making sure that everything you do is legal. There are federal and state laws that provide the operational framework. There are also local district policies that must be implemented effectively and appropriately. Law and policy go hand in hand to provide the basic operational structure of schools (Figure 8.2).

To have the best faculty and staff possible, principals must go beyond the basics. Teachers and other staff members must be recruited, screened, selected, and assigned to positions for which their strengths have best been identified. There is a shortage of certified teachers. We must have a system in place to find the best available and make them want to be part of our team. After all, ours are positive, future-oriented campuses where the focus is on doing what is best for all students. Why should the best and the brightest want to work anywhere else?

Once the best teachers are hired, we cannot just welcome them to the campus, give them the keys, and wish them well. Education is seriously lacking in the area of induction. Induction is more than orientation. It means helping new employees acclimate to the life, culture, campus, and values of the school. It means helping them with the ups and downs of being a new and integral part of the campus. It demands supportive mentoring rather than just well-wishing. It demands taking time and a personal interest in helping them succeed. When teachers succeed, so do students. We have a vested interest in helping all teachers grow and do their best. Part of doing their best is helping them become engaged members of a learning community. In so doing, everyone wins. It becomes a "win-win" situation. I'm all for "win-win" situations—and so are the test developers, so watch for answers that use them on the test.

- *Use formative and summative evaluation procedures to enhance the knowledge and skills of campus staff.*

Figure 8.2   Law and Policy Provide a School's Basic Operating Structure

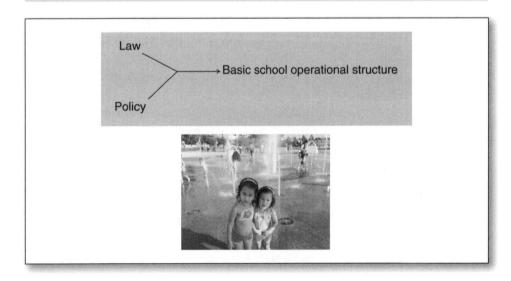

It is morally and ethically wrong to wait until an end-of-the-year summative evaluation to play "gotcha!" with a teacher's assessment. It also isn't fair to the students who are supposed to have been learning from that teacher all along. How can any principal justify that? There should never be any surprises at summative conferences or at contract time if everyone is doing what they should be doing.

So what should they be doing? The best principals are in and out of classrooms all the time. They are there for more than formal evaluations. They are in and out doing walk-throughs. They are in and out saying hello. They are in and out for the sheer pleasure of watching teachers teach and watching students learn. They love every minute of it, just as people who appreciate fine music enjoy really good concerts. To these principals, being in classrooms is not a burden, it is a sheer pleasure. This is why they come to school every day. They do not come to take care of budgets and discipline. They do not come to make sure the buses are running on time. They are not there to calm irate parents. They are there because they get to be engaged in students finding their way in the world through magnificent teaching and learning.

For this to happen, these principals work with teachers, aides, and other staff members on a continuous basis, always looking for ways to enhance curriculum, instruction, programs, facilities, and the learning environment. These are not things that occur easily or overnight. They are nurtured and developed over time. There are no quick fixes. Everything truly valuable develops over time. Think of it like going on a diet. If someone is overweight by 100 pounds and they start a diet, they do not expect to lose it all by next week. They didn't gain the weight overnight, nor will they lose it overnight. What they must do is develop a weight reduction plan, and stick with it. Slowly and with great effort, they begin to lose weight.

The same is true in our schools. Teachers do not develop poor instructional strategies or a bad attitude overnight. Well, sometimes we think they develop a bad classroom climate overnight. But usually it takes time. It will take them time to change. We cannot expect an entire campus to change overnight. We can expect the campus to make slow and steady gains in the right direction, through formative and summative evaluation and feedback, such that incremental gains begin to occur, pick up momentum, and eventually become the new culture of the school. Success breeds success. Praise the tiniest of baby steps forward. Encourage innovation. Celebrate whatever you can find to celebrate until the bigger things start to occur. By using formative and summative evaluation procedures to enhance the knowledge and skills of the campus faculty and staff, teaching, learning, climate, and productivity will be enhanced.

- *Diagnose campus organizational health and morale and implement strategies to provide ongoing support to campus staff.*

As we discussed in Domain I, good culture and climate alone may not make you, but they sure can break you. They are essential to campus organizational health and morale. This is why implementing strategies to

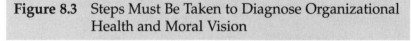

Figure 8.3 Steps Must Be Taken to Diagnose Organizational Health and Moral Vision

provide ongoing support to campus staff is so important. There are various organizational health inventories available on the market today. Likewise, many schools, districts, and regional service centers have developed their own. Each realizes the value and importance of the health and morale of the school.

It isn't enough for a principal to know that the health and morale on his or her campus is pretty good or not so swell. Good principals are always in the process of dreaming up creative ways to implement strategies to provide ongoing support to campus staff. This is part of the stewardship of the vision from Domain I. We must feed the flock. We must nurture those who are in the trenches, day after day, getting the work done. We must provide support for those who are physically or emotionally drained from a particularly exhausting day, week, month, or even a really tough year. It happens. It doesn't mean that you turned into a crummy principal or that your entire staff lost complete reason all at the same time. Sometimes the problem is circumstance. Other times it just seems like plain old bad luck. Some people might argue that there is no such thing as bad luck, that we create our own circumstances. Regardless, it's up to the principal to hold sacred the stewardship of the campus vision and to always look for ways to provide ongoing support by touching the hearts, lives, and minds of all campus staff. In the ideal school, everyone is at his or her best every day. In reality, that probably isn't the case, but it is our goal. It's what we strive for. Our best chance of getting there is to safeguard our organizational health and morale.

- *Engage in ongoing professional development activities to enhance one's own knowledge and skills and to model lifelong learning.*

We have discussed the professional development of all staff members at great length. But what about yours? Who is supposed to nurture and support the principal?

Well, folks, that's a very good question. Some would argue that no one nurtures and supports the principal, that it is a thankless job, and that there is significant truth to the old adage that it's lonely at the top. Too often, this is true. But that will not stop you. You are never to be daunted. You know that others will value what they see you value. You know that your walk must match your talk. Therefore, you desire and look forward to engaging in ongoing professional development activities to enhance your own knowledge and skills and to model lifelong learning.

That sounds like a mouthful, but in truth it is one of the best parts of all the competencies. You want to be actively learning, sharing what you have learned, encouraging others to step out of their own comfort zones, and try new things. They will be more willing to give it a try themselves because they see you doing it. They see you actively, regularly, and enthusiastically sharing what you have learned, what you wish you knew, and how you plan to learn more about whatever interests or will benefit your campus. You are the living, breathing role model of personal professional development. People imitate what they see being practiced successfully. It's been said that imitation is the most sincere form of flattery. This is one place where ego is not the issue. You want them to copy you like crazy! You want them to read, discuss, practice, attend meetings and conferences, reflect, and try new things all the time. What better motivator could they have than a growing, continuously learning principal who is excited to communicate and articulate everything they are learning?

Now, let's discuss professional development from a strictly selfish point of view. In addition to wanting to learn and grow for the benefit of your campus and staff, you want to learn and grow just because you are in love with learning. You will likely be reading a book or listening to a tape the day you die. You are pumped up for learning, and it shows in every facet of your personal and professional life. Your mind is sharp and quick. You are well versed in myriad issues. You can articulate intelligently as a proponent of education for all and on the continued development of a free and democratic society. In other words, you have your act together and are one class act, pardon the pun. Furthermore, you expect the same from students, faculty, and everyone else.

You can participate in growth activities in countless ways. The only limitation is your creativity. Obvious choices are membership and participation in professional organizations on the local, state, and national level. All the educational organizations publish wonderful journals, newsletters, and other media. You receive these simply by being a member. Make it a practice to read something from these every week. You will be surprised how your knowledge of critical issues and the ways they affect your school will improve. Then you can share that knowledge with your campus and facilitate discussion on its relevancy to your school. You can then collaboratively address how to apply it. Conversation and discourse produce a diversity of thought and reflection. Both are good things. Anything that gets people thinking and talking is a good thing—communication builds camaraderie and teamwork; it facilitates the nurturance of the learning community.

The professional organizations also sponsor local, state, and national conferences every year. Students frequently ask me what organization is better, the National Association of Secondary School Principals (NASSP) and its state affiliate, the Texas Association of Secondary School Principals (TASSP), or their elementary counterparts, the National Association of Elementary School Principals (NAESP) and the Texas Elementary Principals and Supervisors Association (TEPSA). They are all excellent, and I'm a member of all of them. If I were still a principal, I would join the one for the area in which I was currently working. Middle school people, you're in luck. All these organizations want you!

In addition to the specific principals' organizations, there are many other worthwhile associations. Two of these are the Association for Supervision and Curriculum Development (ASCD) and Phi Delta Kappa (PDK). Although not specific to principals, both focus on the improvement and timely dissemination of information regarding education. There are others, of course, such as the American Association of School Administrators (AASA) and the Texas Association of School Administrators (TASA), the primary focus of which are superintendents. Nonetheless, many principals and central office people are members of these organizations and benefit greatly from their publications and conferences. The most important thing is not which organizations you join or support, but that you are taking advantage of the opportunities for learning that they provide. You will be surprised at how much your knowledge and expertise increase simply by reading the things they send you in the mail, without ever having to step into a conference. But I strongly encourage you to attend as many conferences as you can. You will benefit physically, cognitively, and emotionally. They will lift you up and recharge you. Can you think of a better reason to attend?

As I said, professional development activities are only limited by your creativity. They can be as simple as visiting a local or nearby school with similar circumstances or demographics or a school that uses a program or teaching strategy in which your campus is interested. Take teachers and other staff members with you. These visits are usually close to home and therefore inexpensive, but they are invaluable. Always remember to share what you have learned. It multiplies the benefits. Plus, it lets your campus know that you did not simply take the day off to have a nice long lunch without them—not that an ideal principal would even think of such a thing. Let teachers see your credibility.

Do all of this until the day you die. Direct your family to have inscribed on your tombstone, "He [or she] lived to learn." Never stop growing and learning. It will keep you sharp. It will keep you from losing focus of what is going on in our field. It will keep you from becoming stagnant.

GUESS MY FAVORITE

It surely will not take a Rhodes Scholar to figure out this one. My favorite is this:

- *Engage in ongoing professional development activities to enhance one's own knowledge and skills and to model lifelong learning.*

If this weren't my favorite, my walk wouldn't match my talk, would it?

IMPORTANT POINTS TO REMEMBER

- Focus all staff evaluation and development activities on helping everyone achieve his or her potential.
- Staff evaluation and development should be from a helpful versus a "gotcha" perspective.
- Time is the common denominator. Without it, other resources cannot be maximized.
- Mentoring and other induction activities are critical to the acclimation of new staff members to the campus culture and values. Help them find their place as an important part of the learning community.
- Make your staff feel appreciated and valued.
- Facilitate ways to retain good people.
- Facilitate growth for all members of the campus community.
- Assessment should occur in every avenue of the school, including personnel. People address what is measured. Help people succeed.
- The stewardship of the vision is your responsibility. Others can and should help, but it is your responsibility.
- Read, study, learn, attend professional conferences, and grow until the day you die.

Learner-Centered Organizational Leadership and Management

Domain II: Instructional Leadership

Domain Key Concepts: Curriculum, Instruction, Staff Development

Competency 007

The principal knows how to apply organizational, decision-making, and problem-solving skills to ensure an effective learning environment.

An effective learning environment is the key to success on every campus. Research in virtually every area of leadership points to the importance of organizational culture and climate to productivity. This concept is stressed in Domain I as well as reiterated in Competency 005. It should come as no surprise that it is also important to organizational, decision-making, and problem-solving skills.

Throughout the domains and competencies, collaboration has been stressed. Collaboration sounds nice, but can it always exist without conflict? No, it cannot. If you have conflict within your school, is that always a bad thing? No, that is not either. Without conflict, there is no diversity of thought. Without diversity of thought, how can we be challenged to confront long-held beliefs that may or may not apply or even be true? How can we grow? How can we address school improvement through change if we have no discourse to prod us to examine our attitudes, viewpoints, and practices? How can we make things better?

Principals should facilitate discussion and collaboration, not dictate it. Principals must lead by example. Remember, good leaders make others want to follow. Respect is not commanded. It is earned. For this to occur, principals must know about, possess, and be able to apply organizational, decision-making, and problem-solving skills. We cannot go into a school and expect things to be rosy all the time. They can't be when schools are filled with imperfect human beings. Interpersonal conflicts will occur. The reason some schools get closer to ideal than others is that their leaders are trained to resolve conflict, to encourage dialogue and innovation, and always to seek better ways of doing things. If we keep on doing what we've always done, we'll keep on getting what we always have.

That's not good enough. To improve, we must read, study, think, reflect, and talk. Collaboratively, we also have to make difficult choices and decisions, deciding which path to take, which curriculum to choose, which instructional strategies are best for individual children, which model of professional development is best for a specific employee, and so forth. These decisions do not always come easily. Often, there are no perfect answers. We must make choices. Sometimes we end up regretting decisions and wishing we could change them. In those cases, it isn't a crime to say, "We messed up," and then go back and readdress the issue. The real crime would be to keep doing something that either isn't working or is just plain wrong simply because "That's my story, and I'm sticking to it." What a pitiful way to run a school. The ideal principal is always formatively and summatively assessing everything to find ways to improve. The ideal principal is never afraid to regroup and do things differently by applying organizational, decision-making, and problem-solving skills to ensure an effective learning environment. There is no other way.

THE PRINCIPAL KNOWS HOW TO . . .

- *Implement appropriate management techniques and group process skills to define roles, assign functions, delegate authority, and determine accountability for campus goal attainment.*

The ideal principal knows there's a fine balance between using a collaborative, open-door leadership style and empowering others in organizational, decision-making, and problem-solving skills. The principal accomplishes this balance by putting specific strategies in place to help others understand their roles within the school community. The ideal principal not only defines roles, functions, and responsibilities but also makes sure team members buy into, understand, and accept them. Authority and acceptance for decision making must be clearly understood such that teachers or others will not "pass the buck," thereby undermining accountability for campus goal attainment.

Remember the old saying, "Be careful what you ask for? You just might get it"? Sometimes that happens when there's a change in leadership style and philosophy. Teachers, staff members, and the community may think they want a collaborative style, yet without appropriate planning, development, training, and implementation, all of it can become a great big bust if they aren't really ready. People need to be sure they want new responsibilities, and then they need to be trained before they can be held accountable for the results. Too often, there are two types of breakdowns that occur:

1. Stakeholders think they want empowerment but realize that with empowerment comes a lot of hard work for which they are unprepared.

2. Stakeholders really do want to be a part of the decision-making process but are not equipped with the skills to be successful.

Therefore, for the organization to be productive and effective, the principal must facilitate an in-depth discussion of the campus vision and of the goals and training to attain that vision. The principal then must provide practice and techniques to ensure those goals are reached.

- *Implement procedures for gathering, analyzing, and using data from a variety of sources for informed campus decision making.*

Well, look here. It's our old pal triangulation again. We are once more trying to look at data from a variety of sources to make prudent, informed decisions based on fact rather than perception, prejudice, or bias. Great principals do not make "seat-of-the-pants" decisions. They do not ask a single person's opinion or look at a single test score or a single anything else. They look at many different sources to make informed decisions. They do this by implementing procedures for gathering, analyzing, and using data from a variety of sources for informed campus decision making.

Figure 9.1 Use Data From Multiple Sources in Decision Making

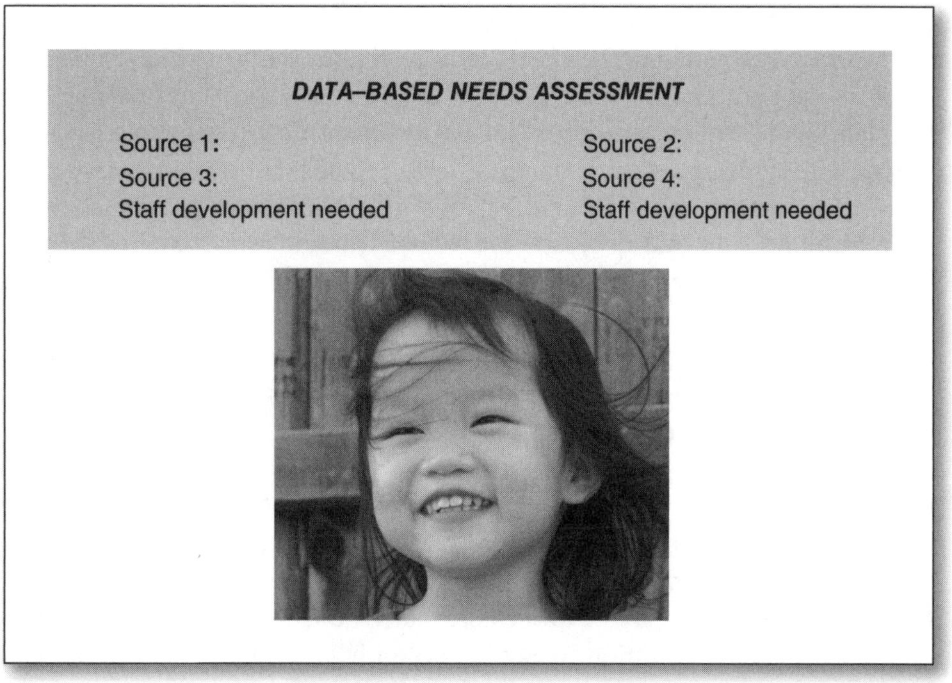

DATA–BASED NEEDS ASSESSMENT

Source 1:   Source 2:
Source 3:   Source 4:
Staff development needed   Staff development needed

- *Frame, analyze, and resolve problems using appropriate problem-solving techniques and decision-making skills.*

Here is another example of integration and overlapping of roles within the principalship. Principals must use various sources of data to make appropriate decisions. They must also use this data to frame, analyze, and resolve problems. To frame a problem means to spell it out, to clearly define it, and to study its different facets to see where the conflicts are. Writing things out is one way to do this. There is something about having to structure thoughts and issues into specific sentences and paragraphs that clarifies them. For this reason psychologists and counselors recommend journal writing as a form of proactive therapy and conflict resolution. It brings things to light, letting you identify problems and brainstorm their solutions in a safe manner. Writing things out helps those involved to analyze the problem and its potential solutions. In analyzing a situation, there are no bad ideas. Everyone's input is welcomed, respected, and considered. All of this comes together to find a healthy way to resolve the problem. If one solution doesn't work, we try another. The important thing is to never give up. We just keep on trying and trying and trying until we get it right. We try not to become discouraged when we fall down. We always remember to get back up. We just keep right on framing, analyzing, and resolving until we come up with the right resolution to solve or improve the problem.

- *Use strategies for promoting collaborative decision making and problem solving, facilitating team building, and developing consensus.*

It all boils down to collaboration. Collaboration is an important sign of a healthy campus culture and climate, as stressed repeatedly in Domain I. We have to talk to each other. No problems were ever solved and no consensus was ever reached by shutting others out and thinking, "The other people at this school are complete idiots. They don't know anything. I must be the only reasonable person here because those others are crazy!"

You and I both know this attitude exists. It may not be that pronounced, but it tends to multiply if given an opportunity. To prevent this, serious planning and resources must be put into the creation of strategies that promote collaborative decision making and problem solving, that facilitate team building, and that develop consensus. Think about Domain I for this one, because it's all about the culture and climate of the school. Planning and resources must be put into developing conflict resolution skills, facilitating the concept of the school as a team, and tools to develop consensus. We may not always agree on everything that happens or even how we will deal with it, but we do agree that this is the plan we're going to try first. All team members will support the plan even if it is not their choice. If it doesn't work, we'll try something else. But for the moment, this is what we have agreed to support. That means we give this idea 100% of our effort. We do not sit back, making only a minimal effort and watching the plan fail, and then smugly say, "I told them that wouldn't work." We turn that negativity into collaboration. We come up with a plan that may not be perfect but that everyone can support and to which everyone will give optimal effort. In so doing, our schools will reap the benefits of collaborative decision making and problem solving, team building, and consensus.

- *Encourage and facilitate positive change, enlist support for change, and overcome obstacles to change.*

We have discussed the concept of the principal as nurturer and cheerleader of the school as well as champion of the stewardship of the vision. How is this done? It's done by knowing that regardless of what happens every single day, you will encourage everyone in a positive manner. You will go beyond encouraging to facilitating, ensuring that change occurs. You will enlist support for change from every element of the school community. You will be on your feet, busy, and proactive. You will not be sitting in your office sipping tea or wondering if the Cowboys will ever get their act together again. In fact, you may have a few things you'd like to share with the Cowboys about team building. Forget the Cowboys and forget sipping tea. There will be days when you do not even have time for lunch and only dream about getting home for supper. You are too busy out in the trenches, encouraging and facilitating positive change, enlisting support for change, and overcoming obstacles to change. There always have been obstacles to change, and there always will be. If we let the obstacles stand in our way, we accept the status quo and thereby say that change cannot occur, that we cannot create a better school, and that we cannot touch lives.

Is that what you really want? Is that what our children deserve? Is that the attitude we need to change the world, one great school at a time? Absolutely not. It's up to us to get out there, get dirty, become physically and emotionally involved, and overcome obstacles. We will not let obstacles be excuses. We want to make Popsicles out of obstacles. We want them to melt on the sidewalks under our feet as we hurry along, making a difference. We will never give up. We will never be defeated. We are positive change agents out changing the world. Those obsolete status quo principals can sit on a tack and bemoan the fate of society. We cannot. We will be the ones to make the difference. We will do this very simply. Every single day we will get out there with everyone we meet to encourage and facilitate positive change, enlist support for change, and overcome obstacles to change. We will develop a thick skin when people tell us we're wasting our time. We will ask them if they have a better way than ours. Somehow I bet that they do not. They are either intimidated or scared to death by our passion. They know that to be a part of our team means work. They will not be able to slough off responsibility at children's expense. At our school, change is in the air, and we are here to make it happen.

- *Apply skills for monitoring and evaluating change and making needed adjustments to achieve goals.*

So while we are on our ongoing quest for excellence, how will we know we are making any progress and not just exhausting ourselves while treading water? We will have a system in place to constantly monitor and evaluate change. What does this mean? It means we will be formatively and summatively engaged in action research. It means we will always ask ourselves and others how we can measure progress or the lack of it. We will establish criteria to measure change and to determine whether that change has been positive or negative.

To do this, we must have a plan. Remember, we do not come up with this plan by ourselves. We must empower our learning team to identify criteria and benchmarks while developing a process to evaluate everything we do on our campuses. If what we are doing works, terrific. But we aren't done. How can we make it even better?

If what we are doing is not working, what really serious things can we do to help it succeed? What can we modify to make it better? After identifying specific strategies, costs must be determined. Are our plans cost-effective? Can we afford them? If not, are there things we can modify to facilitate these methods, ideas, or programs instead of something else? If we cannot afford our new ideas this year, what strategies should we undertake to guarantee that the needed resources are provided for in next year's budget? The most important thing is to always ask ourselves how we can improve everything we do on a daily basis. Is this exhausting? Yes. Will it wear you down? Of course. You are human. But is it necessary to the ultimate productivity of your school as evidenced in the teaching and learning of teachers and students? You bet it is.

GUESS MY FAVORITE

Well, this certainly should come as no surprise. My favorite is the following:

- *Encourage and facilitate positive change, enlist support for change, and overcome obstacles to change.*

If we are not encouragers and facilitators of positive change in our schools, we are in the wrong business. Our schools must have people who are committed to being proactive change agents, enlisting others along the way, and who never let a dumb old obstacle or bureaucrat get in their way. Keep your eyes on the vision. Never give up.

IMPORTANT POINTS TO REMEMBER

- Collaborate!
- Use as many people and as many data sources as possible to empower and make informed decisions. Show me the data!
- Make a system to evaluate, modify, and improve everything. Nothing is exempt. There are no sacred cows. Everything is subject to improvement.
- What is measured gets done. Having a personal program and a goal-attainment accountability system is essential to growth.
- The team is the thing. Schools are joint ventures of multiple people forming a team, a family, with common goals toward the attainment of the campus vision.
- Never, ever, ever, in a billion years give up.

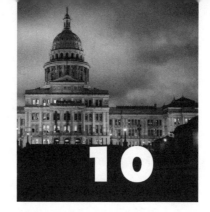

10

The Business and Technology of School Leadership and Management

Domain III: Administrative Leadership

Domain Key Concepts: Finance, Facilities, Student Safety

Competency 008

The principal knows how to apply principles of effective leadership and management in relation to campus budgeting, personnel, resource utilization, financial management, and technology use.

We have now entered Domain III, Administrative Leadership. This is our final domain. It includes Competencies 008 and 009. Both are shorter and more managerial in nature. In fact, the only places you'll find the word management in a competency definition is in Competencies 008 and 009. There is a difference between leadership and management. Leadership looks to the future and is visionary. Management is directed at the daily operation of the organization. Some people are visionary leaders but do not have the skills to manage the details and mechanics of running the school.

Others are the opposite. They are excellent at paper-and-pencil tasks and organization, but they have no vision. Separately, neither is good enough for the ideal school. Today's principal must be a leader and a manager. The ideal principal must be the steward of the school's vision but also able to manage the details of attaining it. This is a classic example of leadership being both a skill and an art. The work of leading and managing, as portrayed in Domain III, is both an art and a skill. Whereas Domains I and II focus on campus leadership, Domain III focuses on campus management. The descriptions in Domain III are short, to the point, and more

Figure 10.1 Competency–Based Principals as Managers

Competency-based principals are good managers as well as good leaders, in relation to

- Campus budget,

- Personnel,

- Resources utilization,

- Financial management, and

- Use of technical equipment.

businesslike in nature than the competencies in Domains I and II. They leave little to interpretation. What they say is what they are. Their key common themes are finance, facilities, and student safety.

In Competency 008, the principal knows how to apply principles of effective leadership and management in relation to campus budgeting, personnel, resource use, financial management, and technology use. It is clear and straightforward. To manage the school, the principal must be a steward of the campus budget, knowing how to collaboratively set goals

Figure 10.2 Strategic Planning

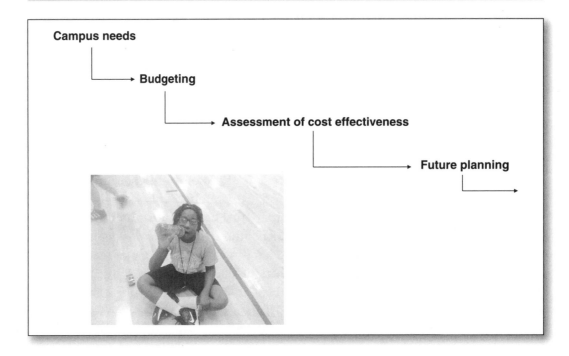

Campus needs

→ **Budgeting**

→ **Assessment of cost effectiveness**

→ **Future planning**

and allocate resources appropriately so that teachers and other staff members have what they need to reach those goals. The principal must plan for appropriate personnel recruitment, retention, and development. The principal must see to it that available resources are used prudently and are cost efficient such that the entire campus budget is solvent. Although technology was previously mentioned in the examples of principal performance, this is the first time it has been directly addressed in the definition of a competency. Technology is of growing importance in both teaching and learning. It is used in various ways, often involving legal regulations. It is the responsibility of the principal to see that it is used efficiently, effectively, safely, and legally.

THE PRINCIPAL KNOWS HOW TO . . .

- *Apply procedures for effective budget planning and management.*

The budget should be planned with collaborative input and be aligned with campus goals (see Figure 3.1). Management of the budget requires consistent prudence in terms of funds and expenditures, as well as legal and policy regulations regarding all curricular and co-curricular accounts. In order for budget planning to be effective it must be based on the needs of the students. Everything we do in schools must be based on the needs of the students. Therefore, everything including the campus vision, goals, culture, climate, curriculum, instruction, assessment, professional development, and safety must be aligned with the needs of the students and, thus, the vision.

- *Work collaboratively with stakeholders to develop campus budgets.*

The campus budget should be developed collaboratively with various stakeholders in the school community. It should not be a well-guarded

Figure 10.3 The Budget and the Vision Must Support Each Other

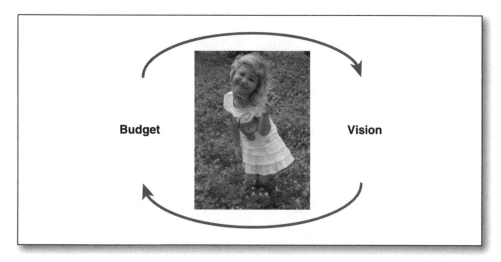

secret kept in the office under strict confidentiality. Goals and priorities for expenditures should be planned and developed together and be aligned with the campus vision. Stakeholders should be empowered in the development, decision making, and utilization of the budget. Nonetheless, the principal is ultimately responsible for the fiscal integrity of expenditures and accountability. Make sure appropriate planning is done so you do not run out of funds in the middle of the year. Plan ahead, and spend accordingly.

- *Acquire, allocate, and manage human, material, and financial resources according to school policies and campus priorities.*

There is more to campus budgeting than money. It is the responsibility of the principal to acquire, allocate, and manage human and material resources as well as financial resources. This includes personnel and curricular resources. All resources must be acquired, allocated, and managed according to school policies and campus priorities as collaboratively developed in the campus vision and school policies.

- *Apply laws and policies to ensure sound financial management in relation to accounts, bidding, purchasing, and grants.*

The principal must apply principles of effective leadership and management in applying laws and policies to ensure sound financial management in all areas. Different schools use different accounting programs and procedures. Each school has its own policies within state and federal regulations. It is the responsibility of the principal to ensure that all laws and policies are consistently and prudently enforced. The test will not ask you accounting questions. It will expect you to keep things legal and within individual school policies.

- *Use effective planning, time management, and organization of personnel to maximize attainment of school and campus goals.*

Having all the material resources in the world will not maximize student learning without effective *time management* and organization. Planning for time management is often overlooked, yet without time to plan, study, develop, conference, and collaborate, no person or campus can maximize attainment of anything. Empower your school community to develop innovative ways to maximize time management. It is an essential component in the attainment of your campus vision.

- *Develop and implement plans for using technology and information systems to enhance school management.*

Where would we be without technology in all its various forms today? The principal must facilitate the development and implementation of plans for using technology and information systems to enhance school management. The Public Education Information Management System, more commonly called PEIMS, is just one type of information system. But it is a major one. Clerical staff members are usually responsible for entering data, but many people are responsible for supplying and checking them. Care must be taken into accurate entry of data into PEIMS. It determines what *Campus Group* your school will be grouped with on your Academic Excellence Indicator System (AEIS) report. You want to be in the right group. This is discussed in greater detail in Chapter 12, "No Data Left Behind." The principal must facilitate technology integration into curriculum and instruction—and throughout the school community. Legal issues, such as site licenses related to the use of designated software on more than one computer, must be consistently applied. Last, and what should be obvious, campus technology should never be used for inappropriate or illegal reasons.

GUESS MY FAVORITE

Now this cannot possibly come as a surprise. My favorite is:

- *Work collaboratively with stakeholders to develop campus budgets.*

IMPORTANT POINTS TO REMEMBER

- Budget development begins with campus goal setting and prioritization.
- Budgets should be developed collaboratively.
- All legal regulations and school policies must be followed consistently.
- Never misappropriate funds!
- If teachers and other members of the school community do not have time to plan, study, and reflect, the campus will not achieve maximum productivity. Time management is critical.
- The use of technology and information systems is essential to school management.

The Physical Plant and Support Systems

Domain III: Administrative Leadership

Domain Key Concepts: Finance, Facilities, Student Safety

Competency 009

The principal knows how to apply principles of leadership and management to the campus physical plant and support systems to ensure a safe and effective learning environment.

There is no greater proof of how much society has changed than when a competency now has to address student and campus safety. In years gone by, school safety was assumed. Only under extremely remote circumstances did deliberate violence occur on school property. When the community thought of school safety, it was in relation to fire and weather drills. If the building and grounds met basic safety standards and appropriate drills were conducted and documented, that was about as far as the issue of school safety was considered.

Unfortunately, this is no longer true. Many schools now have metal detectors. Districts have risk managers. Many, if not most, schools have various types of identification processes for faculty, staff, students, and guests. Visitors must sign in upon arrival and sign out upon departure. Many public school campuses are adopting conservative dress codes or even uniforms in an attempt to reduce disciplinary problems and increase campus pride. Some schools even require see-through purses and backpacks so that weapons or other contraband can be easily seen. Many schools have security guards or campus police at all times, particularly during extracurricular events. Yes, the world has changed. Not all of this change has been good.

We pray that a tragedy like what occurred at Columbine High School, and many other schools and universities, will never happen again. Unfortunately, all the rules in the world cannot solve the underlying causes of school violence. I sincerely wish they could. I sincerely wish there were no need for these rules. I wish every child had a supportive home with parents who supplied them with all the necessities of life, including love, concern, and support. I wish socioeconomic differences, prejudice, bigotry, and other inequities did not exist. But they do.

We cannot prevent all school tragedies. Hoping and wishing will not change the world. Rules will not change the world. All we can do is try—every day and in every way—to make *our* campuses safe and orderly places where teachers can teach and students can learn, where every adult exhibits a sincere interest in every young person, where each person feels valued. We believe in the ideal school. Having the ideal school is a matter of trying to do everything we can with our physical plant, which is our buildings and support systems, such as electricity, gas, and technology, to ensure a safe and effective learning environment for all students and everyone else in the learning community.

Last, what Sherry could we use to define "a safe and effective learning environment"?

School climate. School climate also happens to be one of the top three focus concepts of Domain I. Remember it. It is important.

THE PRINCIPAL KNOWS HOW TO . . .

- *Implement strategies that enable the school physical plant, equipment, and support systems to operate safely, efficiently, and effectively.*

The principal must know how to apply principles of leadership and management to the campus by implementing strategies that enable the school physical plant, equipment, and support systems to operate safely, efficiently, and effectively. In simple language, everything at the school must be safe. The buildings and outdoor spaces must meet all city safety codes. All equipment must operate efficiently and effectively. This encompasses everything from vacuum cleaners to cafeteria equipment, and physical education equipment and life skills equipment. The floors and walls of the school must be clean and safe. There can be no mold or asbestos. The air within the buildings must also be clean and safe. Do not assume it is obvious that everything in the school is safe, efficient, and effective for its designated task.

- *Apply strategies for ensuring the safety of students and personnel and for addressing emergencies and security concerns.*

Think violence, weather, fire, and other disasters, but don't forget other important student safety issues, such as who the custodial parent is, with whom a child can leave the school, and, perhaps more important, with whom a child *cannot* leave the school. Be cognizant of health issues, communicable diseases, and potential allergic reactions. Be sure you have a policy for every type of emergency—from illnesses to broken bones to tornadoes—and then make sure the school community uses that policy. It is your responsibility to ensure the safety of students and personnel and to address emergencies and security concerns. Most important, in the event of any emergency, stay calm. You are in charge. Act that way.

- *Develop and implement procedures for crisis planning and for responding to crises.*

This is another example of why you must have a crisis management plan—and then be ready to work the plan. It does no good to have a plan and then forget to use it during a panic situation. Stay calm. Everyone should have a defined, rehearsed role. In a crisis, everyone should immediately and effectively assume their roles while being on full alert to help others. Student safety is our number one priority, but the safety of the entire faculty and staff is also paramount. You have a crisis management plan. Practice it, hope you never need it, but use it immediately and effectively should the need arise.

- *Apply local, state, and federal laws and policies to support sound decision making related to school programs and operations (e.g., student services, food services, health services, transportation).*

The first rule of thumb in the principalship is to stay legal. Always work within local, state, and federal laws and policies to support sound decision making related to school programs and operations. If you do not stay within these boundaries in every way, unfortunate things are likely to

Figure 11.1   Student Safety Is Paramount

happen. Worse, you'll be unable to improve your school if you cause harm to a person or thing and are either placed on probation or fired. The ideal principal would never get fired.

Examples of school programs and operations include student services, food services, health services, and transportation, but this list is far from definitive. An easy way to remember what to include is to delete the examples and insert the word *all* before school programs and operations. You want to make sound decisions in regard to all programs, operations, and problems. You want to be the wisest principal on the face of the Earth. You want to astound people with your wisdom. You want to live and breathe integrity, ethics, and fairness as described in Competency 003. The first step toward doing this is to always apply local, state, and federal laws and policies. If you are in doubt about the legality of an issue, never be afraid to ask for advice. It is better to ask and have the proper information to make an intelligent decision based on fact than to make a wrong decision based on presumption. It's better to be safe than sorry.

GUESS MY FAVORITE

This one is a complete no-brainer. It is basic to all school and organizational management.

- *Apply local, state, and federal laws and policies to support sound decision making related to school programs and operations (e.g., student services, food services, health services, transportation).*

IMPORTANT POINTS TO REMEMBER

- Stay legal.
- Stay calm.
- Do not be afraid to ask for help.
- A wise decision based on facts is always better than a wrong decision based on presumption.
- Safety for all is paramount to the existence, culture, climate, and vision of the school.
- Have safety and crisis management plans developed, rehearsed, and ready in case of an emergency. Hope and pray you never have to use them.
- Have efficient and effective strategies consistently in place, practiced, and assessed for every facet of the school.

SECTION III

The Real Deal

Practical Application

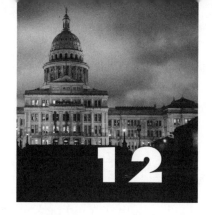

No Data Left Behind

How Do I Read All Those Reports?

DATA ANALYSIS SIMPLIFIED

Being able to analyze data is critical to your success as a principal and in passing either of the administrative TExES exams (principal or superintendent). Yet data analysis remains one of the things that scares test takers. It should not. There are some basic tools to utilize that will help you get a profile of the data. Remember, the TExES exam is built around knowledge and skills that an *entry-level* principal should have. You do not need to know how to disaggregate data for a multivariate statistical doctoral dissertation to pass this test.

HOW TO READ AND INTERPRET STANDARDIZED TEST SCORES

There is no guarantee that you will have a decision set, or any other data to analyze and apply, that is built on standardized tests, their results, or their implications. However, there is also no guarantee that you will *not* either. Some people make a big mistake. They turn the page in their test booklet, see all those graphs, and think, "Here come those awful Academic Excellence Indicator System (AEIS) Reports," or, "Oh, dear. I really hate disaggregating State of Texas Assessments of Academic Readiness (STAAR) test scores," or, "I am an elementary person. What's with all these high school End-of-Course (EOC) test scores?" These people's first response is to panic.

Panicking is not good. As previously shown in Figure 1.1, when anxiety goes up, productivity goes down.

So you are not going to panic. You do not want your productivity to go down. After all, how can you be calm, cool, collected, confident, and almost downright cocky if you are panicking? So, do not panic. Take a deep breath, blow it out slowly, and do what I tell you to do.

Read the prompt for the decision set or data analysis slowly for comprehension purposes. Ascertain what it is really trying to tell you. The prompt will lay the groundwork of what the upcoming questions will be about. It will give you the feel of what the test developers are looking for. There is never anything to panic over in the prompt. All the prompt does is to tell you the direction you are going. So read it and see what you are dealing with. Underline key words. Get the feel of the school you will be analyzing from the way it is described in the prompt.

Once you have done that, look at the charts or graphs provided. Think big picture. At this point, you are *only* interested in the big picture. Standardized tests in these scenarios are usually STAAR or EOC tests. Achievement tests, in various forms, have been around longer than any of our Texas high-stakes tests and are something virtually every campus in the nation either is dealing with or has dealt with. You need to know how to analyze, interpret, and utilize them to increase student performance. These data will provide the parameters to tell you where your schools, as well as each student's, strengths and weaknesses lie. They are crucial for strategic short- and long-term planning.

Look at each chart or graph individually. What is this exact set of data about? What subject is the data referring to? Identify both. Keep breathing slowly, deeply, and confidently. Frankly, you do not *care* what grade or subject the data is about or whether it is elementary or secondary, other than to be prepared for whatever questions may, or may not, be coming your way. Do not think, "Oh, my goodness! These are math scores! I hate math, and I doubly hate math scores!" Do not go there. It will not make one bit of difference if the scores are math, reading, or science, or anything else. Scores are scores. The real question is what are you going to do with them? How are you going to lead and facilitate others to use these data to make informed decisions, also known as data-driven decision making, which will impact the campus vision, curriculum, and instruction? These are the important issues that the TExES exam will want to know that you know how to do. They want to know that you can read the data and that you can analyse them for use in improving student learning. Period. It is all about improving student learning. Nothing else matters. Helping students learn, using every resource possible is what matters.

Next, if you have a chart, look across the top and down the left side to see what your headings are. The headings will provide you with the categories of content that have been tested as well as the rating scales used. Read the concepts the students have been tested on. They likely will be grouped in broad categories. This will provide you the basic overview of what was tested. This helps constitute the big picture that you want to have before you start to read the questions within each decision set. Look next at the rating scales to see how they are categorized.

At this point, you will make some obvious conclusions ranging from "This grade, content area, or campus did pretty well," to "This is horrible. The students do not appear to be learning much of anything. I need to be in charge of this school to turn it around!" You may notice some particular areas where the grade, content area, or campus did very well, or some areas where they did particularly bad . . . which is a polite way of saying they stunk. More likely, the majority of their scores will be somewhere in between.

This is important. As shown in Figure 12.1, high scores, or scores that are moving upward, are *campus strengths.* Low scores, or scores that are moving downward, are *campus weaknesses.* High scores are good. Low scores are bad. Every school has both strengths and weaknesses. However, one school's weakness may be another school's strength. You are interested in:

- On the day of the test, the school presented in the decision set
- In the future, the school where you are the ideal principal moving your campus from reality toward ideal

Having said that, this is a high-stakes test for you so, sometimes, your nervous instinct will be to play the "What If? Game." No. Nowhere in this book will I tell you to try to second guess what the test developers may ask you. Do not try to be psychic with the potentially mass of data by thinking, "What if they ask me something I don't know? What else can I conclude from these data? What *could* they ask me? Oh, my goodness. I do not even know what these concepts stand for! What if they ask me something I am clueless about?" While you are, thus, playing the "What If? Game," two things are happening:

- Your anxiety level is going up. We all know by now what happens when your anxiety level goes up. We do not want that. Definitely not! We do not want your anxiety level so low, as evidenced by regular huge sighs, that people around you think you are on Prozac. Leave the "What If?

Figure 12.1 Identifying Campus Strengths, Weaknesses, and Trends

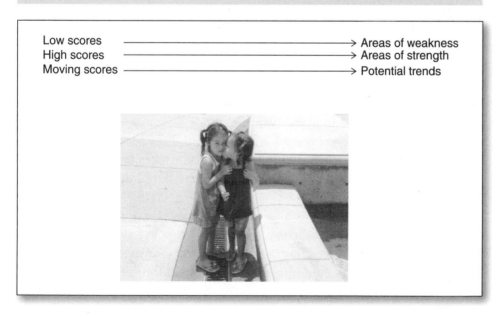

Low scores ——————————————→ Areas of weakness
High scores ——————————————→ Areas of strength
Moving scores ————————————→ Potential trends

Game" alone. I will give you plenty of *productive* techniques in the next chapter. Right now, just identify the broad categories the data represent, and move on. Do *not* try to read the minds of the test developers regarding what they may ask. After all, they got paid for developing the test. You did not. Your job is to pass the test.

- The clock is ticking. You have plenty of time to take and pass this test. However, it makes no sense to waste the time you have. There is no reason for you to sit there, staring at all that data while playing the "What If? Game." You do not want to *wonder*. You want to *know*. Thus, while you are wondering what they *might* ask you, the clock is ticking away your precious minutes. No, no, no! You are not going there. Turn the page. Go see what they *are* asking rather than fretting over *What If?* It is a better utilization of your limited time, keeps you on track and focused, and keeps you working *with* the clock rather than against it.

Remember, in your initial view of the data, all you want to do is get the essence of what it is presenting, such as grade, subject, basic concepts tested, and an overview of how the grade, content area, or campus performed.

Next, turn the page, and get started on the actual questions. This test is a mind game. Do not let it psych you out. Beat it at its own game. Keep reading, answering, and turning those pages.

The Pleasant Surprise

Here is the *pleasant* surprise. In an entire decision set, rarely will they ask more than two to three questions that will actually require you to go back and *look* at the data. The rest of the questions will be generic in nature, similar to questions in any other decision set. But, if you are hyped up over what they *might* ask you, you could miss the basic questions. That is the surprise benefit of not getting yourself worked up or playing the "What If? Game." Just go see what they really *are* asking. This keeps your anxiety down, your productivity up, and the clock as your friend instead of your enemy.

When you do come to the questions that actually have you look at the data, you do not have to be a statistical whiz. They are looking for *entry-level* data analysis knowledge and skills. Therefore, if they ask you where a large or the larg*est* need in the campus, grade, or content area is, look for the *lowest* scores or those on a downward trend. Low scores indicate need for improvement. As shown in Figure 12.1, downward trends indicate we are going the wrong direction and require immediate intervention to turn them around.

Even the best campus has a low area in *something*. Until *every* student at every school has 100% mastery of *every* concept on every test, there is always a need to improve. Having 100% mastery means all students are learning. This includes students with various disabilities as well as language, economic, and cultural differences. It represents an ideal situation.

Remember, the ideal principal is all about *every* student doing well and the campus being on a constant move toward becoming ideal. Doing this is a classic example of being a reflective and data-sensitive leader. Every principal, teacher, and member of the campus community must continuously ask themselves and others, "How can we do *everything* better?" This is called using data for continuous student learning improvement. It makes no difference if we are discussing math scores, band competitions, or the Pillsbury Bake-Off. Until every student masters every objective, we are not there yet. We are not through seeking improvement. We do not have time to rest on our laurels and think as Scarlet O'Hara did, "I'll think about it tomorrow at Tara." We must lead our schools *today* to prepare educated, informed, and productive citizens necessary for the American democratic society of tomorrow.

However, we cannot wait until tomorrow to think about the difficult tasks ahead of us. We cannot procrastinate. We must always and forever be asking, "How can we do this better?" Identify it, and do it. There are no excuses. Excuses are for losers. *You* will lead your students, faculty, and other stakeholders to know that they are *winners*. There is no time to waste. To enhance student performance as measured by standardized test scores, you must know how to read, analyze, draw conclusions about, and facilitate the implementation and assessment of programs, curriculum, instructional strategies, and personnel that will meet the needs of today's students in your campus. Do not focus unduly on what is working elsewhere. That is not your job. Your job is to create the best organizational culture and climate to facilitate maximized student performance in your campus. As shown in Figure 12.1, the answers to where the areas are to address are in the data. Every school has different strengths and weaknesses. Your role is to know your data inside out, to be able to speak fluently and coherently about them to anyone who will listen, and to always be thinking of new and better ways to engage and enhance student learning.

Therefore, refer back to Figure 12.1 yet again. If a question steers you toward areas of *growth* within a campus, grade, or content area, you will look at the numbers to see the greatest difference in a *positive*, not a negative direction. If a question asks you where schools greatest strengths are, look for the *bigger numbers* or the areas showing the *greatest upward trends*. It could be that one category of concepts or a certain grade is still higher than another, *but* those scores are stagnant or even regressing a tiny bit. At the same time, another area may be showing consistent, steady, albeit slow, growth. If the numbers are consistently coming up, even if it is slowly, that is a positive thing and should be noticed, praised, and supplemented. Watch for answers that catch trends like that. The test developers love to throw in responses that determine if you are utilizing higher order thinking skills by catching trends or implications. Show them you are by selecting the correct response.

You will not be asked any detailed or advanced statistical analysis questions. That is not the primary role of the principal and certainly not a beginning principal. The test will not ask you about variances or standard deviations, so relax. They do want to know that you know how to determine if students in your campus are learning, what their individual and collective strengths and weaknesses are, and that you are leading planning processes to increase student performance for *all* students based on the scores presented. If students from *all* subgroups are not learning, why aren't they? What can be done to improve the culture, climate, instruction, and curriculum of the campus such that *all* students can and do learn? Therefore, the purpose of any testing is threefold. The purpose is to:

- measure student growth;
- assess student and campus strengths, weaknesses, and trends; and
- use data as a valid means of determining goals for student growth and improvement for the campus, grade, subgroups, and content areas.

Last, remember, it does not matter how high the preponderance of your students' scores are, if *everyone* is not learning. This test is about *all* students, not just some of them. Ideal principals never, ever, ever give up until *every* student is mastering every concept. Campus excellence is not determined simply by the scores of students who are motivated and easy to teach. Campus excellence is determined by the success of *all* students in *all* areas. Excellence is for *everyone*. Do you think this philosophy is unrealistic? Fine. It may be. But we do not care about realistic. We care about ideal. There are other jobs available for those who lose sight of the ideal. Places outside education are hiring. They have plenty of jobs for those who only want a paycheck and do not have a passion for excellence in learning for everyone to further the promulgation of an enhanced American democratic society. As for you, you are on your own quest for educational excellence. If you are not on this quest, on the day of the test, *pretend* you are! This test is about excellence for all. *If you do not truly believe this can be attained, you will not pass this test.* If you do believe all students can and will learn provided they have the right curriculum, instruction, resources, and support services, you are on your way to being a cutting-edge, highly effective principal.

HOW TO READ AND INTERPRET AN "ACADEMIC EXCELLENCE INDICATOR SYSTEM" REPORT

Whereas students all across America in both public and private schools take achievement tests, the AEIS is exclusive to Texas. Every district and campus is rated by this important accountability system based largely on data detailed in the annual AEIS report. Two important areas are student passing rates on the STAAR and EOC exams and student attendance. However, do not be surprised if you see references to their precursor, which was called the Texas Assessment of Knowledge and Skills (TAKS).

Some questions or decision sets may have not yet been updated. This will have no impact on how you answer questions since each of the tests is built around increasing student performance for all students.

As you begin looking at any AEIS report, first look at the overall report to see what you have been presented. There are *three specific areas* to consider. You may or may not be given each of these areas to analyze, but you want to know about all of them, just in case. First is the cover or title page. It will tell you the academic year of testing, as well as the name, campus number, and state rating of the overall campus.

The subsequent AEIS report is divided into two sections. There are certain things that always appear in each section and never are changed. Memorize them. Please notice this is the first time I have asked you to memorize anything. I did not ask you to memorize any of the nine competencies. I asked you to fully understand and comprehend them so you would recognize what the test developers are questioning you about. Yet, now I am asking you to memorize what is in Section I and what is in Section II. Doing this will save time and anxiety in searching through a report to find the data you need to make informed responses to your test questions.

As shown in Figure 12.2, the simplest way to remember where data are located is to know that everything about *testing and attendance* is in Section I. Everything about testing that you can think of, as well as *attendance,* is in Section I. There is nothing else there. *Everything else is in Section II.*

Remember that.

Therefore, when determining where to look for an appropriate answer, if the question has anything to do with test scores or student attendance, you know the answer will be in Section I. You can, thus, ignore Section II for this question.

Figure 12.2 Components of an AEIS Report

SECTION I:

Test data
Attendance

SECTION II:

Student information (except testing)
Staff information
Budget information
Program information

However, if the question does not relate to testing or student attendance, go straight to Section II. Look in the appropriate category there. Section I always and forever will only have information regarding student performance and attendance, so your answer will not be there. For ease in navigating the report, the section and page numbers are listed in the top right corner of each page. Now let's look deeper into what these things mean.

Section I of an AEIS Report: Student Testing Data

The first section of the AEIS report addresses everything you would ever want to know, or not want to know, about student performance on TAKS, or shortly, STAAR. It is presented in a chart format. STAAR, and formerly TAKS, begins in the third grade and continues through Grade 8. It was originally given primarily in reading, math, and writing with secondary schools also reporting EOC test results. Subsequently, tests in both science and social studies were added. Some subjects, such as writing, science, and social studies, are not given in every grade; thus, there will not be any scores reported for the grades in which they are not given. Currently, STAAR is not given on the secondary level. Secondary EOC exams are currently given in 12 areas. These are English I, English II, English III, Algebra I, Algebra II, Geography, World Geography, World History, U.S. History, Biology, Chemistry, and Physics. Test results are reported in Section I because all testing information is in Section I, regardless if it is elementary or secondary.

The student groups are listed at the top of the chart from left to right with the largest subgroup coming first and going in decreasing size to the various demographic subgroups. For the sake of our discussion, let's say that we are presented with an AEIS report that is looking at third-grade reading and math scores, since writing is not given in the third grade. It is helpful to think "big to little" in looking at each subgroup and how it performed. Individual student scores are never known on either a campus or campus AEIS report. Individual student performance is provided on the campus level and protected by privacy laws. In other words, while you may go online to see how any campus or district in Texas did on their AEIS report, you cannot determine how Little Johnny Next Door did on his tests. It will not be there. If you are asked any question that seeks to check your knowledge of student privacy and confidentiality, the answer is the public does *not* get to see or access individual student records.

The biggest group is the *State,* so state results will appear in the first column. Under this column, the scores of students per grade and subject are provided. In our example of third grade, the column will show how all third graders in Texas did on reading and math. Everyone, and especially the press, wants to compare and contrast how your campus did in comparison to the overall state. No one wants to be below the state average in any area.

The next column is the *Campus Group.* The *Campus Group* is also exceedingly important. It is second in importance only to the column that is your *Campus.* What is the *Campus Group?* Each year, detailed demographic data about every student in every campus as well as data about the campus itself are entered by staff (not you, thank goodness) into the Big State Computer in the Clouds called the Public Education Information Management System (PEIMS). The Big State Computer in the Clouds crunches all the numbers and codes for various factors such as race, gender, student age, grade, socioeconomics, mobility, campus wealth, and so forth. Each campus is subsequently given an opportunity to correct erroneous information at specific points during the year to assure data accuracy. As a principal, it is in your best interest for this information to be perfect because this is what is used to determine your *Campus Group*. The *Campus Group* includes the schools in the state that are the *most similar* to yours according to all the factors indicated above for PEIMS. You want to be in the correct campus group because your campus's performance will be compared and contrasted to these fine folks in your good old AEIS report.

You may wonder why that is such a big deal. Let me explain it to you. Let's say that you are principal of Poor Me Middle School. Poor Me MS is, gee, rather pitiful. For example, 100% of the students are eligible for free or reduced-priced lunch. No one speaks English. No one lives in a single-family dwelling. In fact, virtually everyone lives in low-rent property and moves all the time. Thus, students at your school are constantly changing and rarely get to establish many roots. Few of the homes have two parents in them. Unemployment, alcohol, and drugs abound. For the sake of discussion, I am overexaggerating, but you get the point. Poor Me MS has had dismal scores on all forms of student testing for years and has earned sympathy from everyone because, gee, they are a rather pitiful lot. Who could expect them to perform very well academically? They have been pitiful and gotten by with it without too much protest. Poor Me MS is your classic example of low expectations and reaping what you sow. If you do not think a student or campus will produce much, guess what: They won't. Fortunately, the opposite is also true. If we know that to be true, why do we not expect high performance out of everyone?

Well! The *Campus Group* addresses that. Poor Me MS is now being compared to *other* schools whose demographics look just like theirs. What principal would want to have to explain to the superintendent, school board, or the community why its students perform worse than other schools that look *just like them* and have almost identical circumstances? The net result is, when the *Campus Group* category was added to AEIS reports, scores went up at all schools—including Poor Me schools. Welcome to the age of high-stakes accountability in a No Child Left Behind world.

Let's move on.

Now that you have done such a good job improving student performance as principal of Poor Me MS, you have been solicited to apply, and ultimately get, the principal position at Pretty Good High School. Pretty Good HS is in the same geographic area as Poor Me ISD, but that is all they have in common. At Pretty Good ISD, there is no rental property. Everyone owns their home and is proud of it. Everyone speaks English and maybe another couple of languages just for fun. No one qualifies for free or reduced-priced lunch. There is virtually no mobility. In fact, parents of kindergarteners are already requesting the teachers they want their children to have in first, second, or third grade! Almost every home has two parents plus maybe a maid or a nanny. No one rides the bus because children walk or ride their bikes safely to school, or neighborhood car pools pick them up to take them to scouts, soccer practice, gymnastics, or piano lessons. Along the way, they stop and have a snow cone or ice cream. Life is so nice at Pretty Good HS. Not surprisingly, so are the test scores. They are pretty good.

But they are not *excellent*. Administrators, faculty, staff, and even the school board members at Pretty Good ISD have been content with the high school campus's pretty good scores. After all, they *always* outperform those poor, pitiful little children over at Poor Me ISD, God bless them. Here at Pretty Good ISD, students can do relatively well without too much extra effort. They look pretty good under the *State* and *Campus* columns, so what is the problem?

That is where the *Campus Group* comes in handy. Now scores from Pretty Good HS are being compared to scores from other pretty good high schools that look just like them. Oops! What principal would like to explain to the superintendent, school board, and community why, although their scores are pretty good, they are *below* their *Campus Group* of other schools that look virtually just like them? This would not be a happy conversation. Therefore, instruction at all the pretty good campuses also becomes much more focused and data driven. The result is improved curriculum, instruction, and assessment in the Pretty Good, Poor Me, and all other campuses in the state. Although some consider the *Campus Group* a headache, it actually is a good thing. It keeps all schools on their toes and cognizant of how other schools with similar demographics are doing. The net results are improved learning and accountability for everyone. In simple language, the *Campus Group* holds all of us accountable for teaching and learning every day. If a principal is not leading and facilitating improved student learning for truly altruistic reasons, the AEIS report should take care of it.

The *Campus* column is, obviously, your own campus's scores. Although it is not the first column in the "big to little" sequence, it is the first column you look at because, honey, it is yours. State law now requires student performance scores from the campus AEIS report to be used in the principal's annual evaluation. Believe me, the scores presented here are of the utmost importance to your job security. To facilitate easy reading, highlight your scores in yellow. Study and think about them almost 24 hours a day. These data should be critical elements in guiding all subsequent analysis and discussion of campus needs and goal setting. How will you lead your campus personnel, as well as the community, to improve student performance based on these and campus-level data? What are other important sources of data that should be included in campus strategic planning?

After the *Campus* column, still thinking "big to little," the columns are divided into various student subgroups. These include African American, Hispanic, White, American Indian, Asian/Pacific Islanders, Male, Female, Economically Disadvantaged, and Special Education. The goal is for every subgroup to do well, including Special Education. You do not want to see any large differences in passing rates of students on any section of any test. If you do, you and your stakeholders must ask why *all* of your students are not performing well. Then create plans and strategies to resolve the discrepancies. In the ideal campus, instruction is individualized and curriculum is developmentally appropriate such that there will be no significant deviations between subgroups. When, in reality, there are deviations, intense study and planning are undertaken by many stakeholders to resolve the situation such that all students learn with maximized performance for their varying ability levels. This is not simply an idealistic philosophy. It is reality in today's schools.

Those are all of the categories placed into columns. Along the left side of each page in Section I are rows labeled with the subjects tested such as reading, math, writing, science, social studies, or *All Tests*. Appropriate scores will be noted on two lines for the current year and the previous year. In each area, you will want your scores to be coming *up* annually, not going down. If they are going down or remaining stagnant, again, you and your campus-community must analyze *why* and plan for both short- and long-term improvement.

The *All Tests* is an interesting row. It is there to determine the percentage of students who passed every test they took. It is necessary because if you just looked at the individual subjects and compared results, you would get a less than complete picture. For example, let's go back to our hypothetical set of campus third-grade scores. Say 50% of the third graders passed reading, and 50% of the third graders passed math. At first glance, you might think, "Well, 50% of the students in third grade are doing really well. The other 50% cannot read nor do math."

This could be a wrong conclusion. What if it was a *different* set of students that passed each portion?

- What if 50% of them actually have the ability to read *War and Peace* but could not successfully add 2 + 2?
- What if the other 50% could work algorithms but could not read *The Cat in the Hat?*

Hmm. We have a problem here. This problem is why we have the *All Tests* row. It allows us to see an overall picture of exactly what percentage of the campus is passing *everything* taken. The goal is to have 100% of the students passing all tests.

The first portion of Section I will always be set up in this format. Therefore, this is where you would look if you were asked any questions that relate to specific grade-level or subgroup performance on any test for any grade or for the campus as a whole. If you are asked to compare scores, ascertain trends, or identify strengths or weaknesses of performance, this is also where you would look.

The next portion of Section I is a summary of all the scores in the campus. The rows and columns of the chart remain the same. It will say *TAAS/TAKS % Passing Sum of 3–8 & 10*. If the campus you are analyzing is quite small and does not have all those grades, it does not matter. This chart is simply a quick reference guide to the overall performance of how the entire campus did on the specified subjects and *All Tests*. If you are asked any questions about overall campus performance, this is where you would look first.

At the bottom of this portion is an important section labeled *Exempted Sum of 3–8*. This is important because although it will be wonderful if you have 100% passing rates in every category above, if you have exempted half the campus, it is not a good reason why. Superintendents, school boards, as well as the state itself, look at this closely. They do not want you exempting high percentages of students. Their goal is for everyone to test and score well. Therefore, this section will show the percentage of students, per subgroup, that you have exempted for any reason, including special education or limited English proficiency (LEP) purposes. Again, it is *very important* for you to have low percentages in this area. Special education students must now test in alternative ways, and scores are reported. *Exemptions* are one of the few places that you want your numbers to be *less* than the *State, Campus,* or *Campus Group*. You particularly do *not* want high percentages of exemptions or bad scores within any of your subgroups. Again, the goal is for everyone to test and everyone to do well. We want *all* students to learn and learn well, even if they are difficult to teach.

Section I of an AEIS Report: Student Attendance

The last portion of Section I is *Attendance*. Attendance is important because if students are not coming to school, it is difficult for them to maximize their learning opportunities . . . or at least the things you want them to learn. The same format for grouping columns previously described is also used here. The important thing to notice is that the two years listed are always one year behind. That is not an accident, nor is it placed there to confuse you. The reason is simple. This academic year is not over yet; therefore, it is impossible to determine the total percentage of attendance. Obviously, you want your attendance percentages to be *higher* than your *State* or *Campus Group*. You do want to see high attendance percentage rates among all campus subgroups. If a certain subgroup has low attendance, it is critically important to ascertain *why*. Why are these students not coming to school? What can we as a campus or community do to address this situation? Again, if students are not in attendance, it is going to be very difficult for them to learn. Also, since this is Texas, and we have a rule or regulation for everything, if attendance becomes too low or dropout rates become too high, the campus will be cited by the State with very serious consequences. These consequences, if not addressed, could result in the campus receiving bad ratings, being put under a state "master" for leadership, or ultimately being closed. Needless to say, these are not things any campus wants to have happen. A major goal of a democratic society is to produce literate, cognizant, contributing citizens. This is hard to do when students are not in school.

Section II of an AEIS Report

A simple way to remember what is in Section II is that it has everything that is *not* in Section I. While that may appear obvious, it is very easy to remember the two things that are in Section I. They are student testing and student attendance. Therefore, if you are asked a question that does *not* relate to testing or attendance, go straight to Section II. A quick reminder hint is that if you ever get lost in the pages of an AEIS report, the quickest way to find out where you are is to look at the top right corner of each page. It will say if you are in Section I or Section II. Let's now see what *is* in Section II. We already know it is *not* testing or attendance information!

The first segment of Section II is *Student Information*. Everything is still presented in chart format. The subgroups no longer appear. The basic layout will be *Campus, Campus Group*, and *State*. You will be given basic student enrollment (*not testing*) information such as how many students and what percentage of your enrollment is in each grade and school of the campus. It will be further disaggregated into *Ethnic Distribution, Mobility, Economically Disadvantaged, Limited English Proficient, Number of Students per Teacher*, and *Retention Rates*. This will be charted in rows comparing this campus to their *Campus Group* and the *State*. Other than *Number of Students per Teacher* and *Retention Rates by Grade* for both regular and special education students, there is no doing better or worse than these groups here. These are merely facts. However, you would like to see a small ratio of students to teachers as well as a *small* percentage of student retention. Although this section does not relate to testing, it is an important place to look when you are analyzing a report. Just as you do not want high passing rates due to high exemption rates, you also do not want high passing rates due to flunking everybody (found in this portion of Section II). This is the kind of critical thinking that test developers like to see if you will catch. Watch for it. We want everyone doing well on STAAR and EOCs, of course, but *not* because the campus exempted or flunked everyone at risk of not passing the test. Basically though, if you are given a question that pertains to *Enrollment, Ethnic Distribution, Mobility, Economically Disadvantaged, Limited English Proficiency, Number of Students per Teacher*, or *Retention Rates by Grade* for either regular or special education students, then the *Student Information* chart of Section II is where you would look. Remember this is where to find it for test-taking day.

The next section of Section II is *Staff Information*. It is set up in the same *Count, Percent, Campus Group*, and *State* format as *Student Information*. This is where you will look to determine numbers and percentages of staff that are *Professional* (teachers, professional support, and campus administration), plus *Educational Aides, Total Staff, Total Minority Staff, Teachers by Ethnicity and Sex, Teachers by Years of Experience, Average Years of Experience of Teachers, Average Years of Experience of Teachers with Campus, Average Teacher Salary by Years of Experience,* and *Average Actual Salaries* for teachers, professional support, and campus administration. These data are public information and freely available to any citizen who wants to see them either by hard copy or via the Internet. The AEIS report brings various data together in one report.

If you are asked any questions regarding average salaries for virtually anyone, this is where you would look. If you were asked questions that involve planning for future personnel needs, one place to check would be to look at the average years of experience of campus staff to begin thinking about future retirements and their potential effect on staffing, the budget, and instruction. This is where you would look to see how well your campus is doing in comparison to the others in recruiting and retaining minority staff. This is a pressing issue for all schools. Because this is such a common issue statewide, watch for it as a common theme that could appear on the test.

For virtually any question you may have that relates to staffing, the *Staff Information* segment within Section II is where you would look first. Always think, "Is there any place else I could look for something that could be of importance to answering this, or any, question?" Remember, the competencies refer to using multiple sources of data repeatedly. By becoming familiar with exactly where to find what you're looking for in the AEIS report, you can utilize multiple pieces of information from within the same document to make an intelligent, data-driven decision.

The next component in Section II is *Actual Operating Expenditure Information*. This is where you will find everything about the budget in a summarized form. The format will again compare the *Campus, Campus Group,* and *State.* A rule of thumb is that principals, superintendents, school boards, and especially taxpayers like test scores to be *higher* than anyone else's, but for the campus to be doing it with *less* money. Using that rationale, this, plus student retention and the teacher/student ratio, are the places you would like your numbers to be *less* than your comparison groups. The first place was in Section I in *Exempted Sum of 3–8.* We discussed it again in *Number of Students per Teacher* and *Retention Rates by Grade.* When it comes to money, always look for financial *prudence.* This is particularly true in relation to administrative costs. Boards and taxpayers like to see money targeted directly toward students and instruction and as little as possible toward administration. Within the *Actual Operating Expenditure Information* you will find the actual amount and percentage of the budget for the *Total Campus Budget* by *Function* and *Per Pupil.* Think, "Scores up, costs down." Remember this when looking at both budgets and test results. Remember this especially on the day you take your TExES exam.

The last chart in Section II is *Program Information.* This is where you will find how many students are in each category of the campus program as well as the amount of money spent on each. *Program Information* uses the consistent Section II chart format of columns for *Count, Percent, Campus Group, Campus,* and *State.* The rows then provide the categories. These are *Student Enrollment by Program* for *Special Education, Career & Technology Education, Bilingual/ESL Education,* and *Gifted & Talented Education.* It provides the numbers and percentages of *Teachers by Program* for *Regular, Special, Compensatory, Career & Technology, Bilingual/ESL, Gifted & Talented,* and *Other.* Next, it details the *Budgeted Instructional Operating Expenditures by Program* for each. If you are asked questions about program equity, particularly in the area of finance, this would be where you would first look.

My last suggestion for you in data analysis is to utilize your common sense. Think prudently. Improving student performance is your guiding principle in every instance. That is what they are looking for, so show it to them in your answer choices.

SUMMARY

In closing our study of data analysis through standardized tests and AEIS reports, remember to do these things:

- Look to see the profile of what you have been given. What kind of test or what portion of an AEIS report has been provided for your review?
- What concepts or components are made available?
- Do *not* play the "What If? Game." Do *not* try to be psychic by trying to draw conclusions about the data *before* you read each question. Turn the page, and *read* the questions. Then you will know where to look and what to analyze per question.
- The test is looking only for *entry-level* data analysis skills. Keep your anxiety level down so your productivity will stay *up.*
- Practice looking at various standardized test results and AEIS reports within your own campus or on the Internet before the TExES exam so that you will be familiar and comfortable with forms and layout.
- Memorize what goes in Sections I and II of an AEIS report. This will save you time and anxiety on the day you test because you will know exactly where to look for the answers.

Assuming you have one or more decision sets relating to an AEIS report, look to see if you have a Section I, Section II, or both. Similar to standardized test results, you will look at the overview of what you have been given. The top right corner of every page will provide this information. You can easily remember what types of information will be found in *Section I.* It is basically *testing and attendance. Everything else* is in *Section II.* Go directly to the questions to see exactly what they are asking rather than playing the "What If? Game" of what they *might* ask. This saves time, effort, and anxiety.

Knowing and becoming familiar with the *format* of an AEIS report, plus knowing what will always be in Sections I and II, turns a scary and sometimes formidable portion of the TExES exam into a very workable passage. Remember, Section I has testing and attendance. Everything else is in Section II. Knowing this and making yourself familiar with multiple AEIS reports from various campuses before the test will help you walk into your test *cool, calm, collected, confident, and almost downright cocky.* This confidence level is what you want as you *ace* this test.

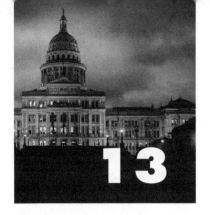

Test-Taking
Strategies

Now Listen to Me Here . . .

It is assumed that students who are preparing for the principal TExES examination have had an appropriate university or alternative preparation program in school leadership. The goal of this book is to enhance that foundation and to help you pass the TExES examination. The purpose is not to reteach your masters degree or certification program. Therefore, assuming you have the prerequisite knowledge base necessary *and* you utilize the philosophy and skills presented in this book, you should *ace* this test. That means you should be able to walk in to take the TExES exam cool, calm, collected, confident, and almost downright cocky. Anxiety is not your friend. As shown earlier in Figure 1.1, when your anxiety goes up, your productivity goes down. The reverse is also true.

The test, from this point on, is a mind game. You have the knowledge and conceptual framework to knock the top out of this test. Therefore, what you think you will achieve, you will achieve. If you think you will pass the test, you will. If you think you will not, you won't. Either way, you will be right. Your mind is the front wheel of the wheelbarrow that leads your life. Go forward with a positive mind-set. Here are strategies to help you.

THE TESTING SESSION: GENERAL OVERVIEW

Organizational guru Stephen Covey (1990) reminds us to sharpen the saw before we begin virtually anything. In this instance, the time you spend studying, analyzing, sorting, and organizing your data is sharpening your saw. It will be time very well spent before you begin answering the test questions. If you do not spend this time effectively and efficiently, you will lose productivity during the remainder of the session, as you have to go back and read the question again to find what is needed to answer the questions appropriately. If you keep these things in mind, once you begin addressing the questions, you will have the big picture of the school already in your mind. Reading a question well, for comprehension of what they are really asking you, is not a waste of time. It is your key to success in picking the best responses. Sharpen your saw well. Remember always, to respond to these questions as

- an ideal principal,
- making data-driven and student-focused decisions,
- aligned with the theoretical framework (three domains and nine competencies),
- using the 1–2–3–4 Plan,
- "The Process" for multiple-multiples, and
- watching for the key concepts, such as the "Sherry list" first shown in Figure 2.2.

Analytical and Problem-Solving Skills

Your exam will consist of multiple-decision sets similar to what you experienced on the Principal Practice TExES exam. Each decision set is composed of a prompt, followed by related questions. When you begin this section, read the prompt that introduces the first decision set. Remember, there are no questions or answers in the prompt. The prompt simply tells you a little bit about the school or situation you will be addressing. As you read, underline words that you think are important. You are allowed to write in your test booklet. You do not get bonus points for turning in a clean booklet, so use your visual and kinaesthetic senses by underlining key words or important concepts throughout TExES. This will help you stay focused on what the question is really asking and not allow you to become distracted by potentially great responses that do not happen to answer *this* question.

There are specific strategies that will help you. Thus far, you have studied hard for the principal TExES exam. Now it is time to learn other test-taking techniques to help you win this mind game and, subsequently, knock the top off this test.

THE DOT GAME: A PSYCHOLOGICAL AND TIME MANAGEMENT STRATEGY

You will have plenty of time to successfully complete this exam. There is no reason for you to run out of time. However, on rare occasion, I hear of someone who claims they did. I am going to teach you to utilize a deceptively simple technique called The Dot Game. If you play The Dot Game, it is impossible for you to run out of time. Here is how to do it.

After reading the prompt for your first decision set, you will read the first question. You will mark the answer. You will read the next question. You will mark the answer. This will go along just fine until you get to a question where you really are not sure of the answer. This question is one of those that make you go, "Hmmmmm." This happens to everyone, so do not feel bad. Read the question and possible answers again. If you still do not feel confident about which is the correct response, put a dot by the question and move on. Just skip that question. Do not feel guilty. Do not look back. Just put the dot by it and keep on moving. Don't worry. The Dot Game has steps. You will come back to this question, and any others you leave a dot by, later.

Continue until you hit another question where you are not sure of the answer. Put a dot by it, too. Do not spend over two minutes pondering the right answer to any question. The longer you spend trying to figure out the answer, the more your anxiety level will go up. When your anxiety level goes up, your productivity goes down. Worse, the clock is ticking. The clock is not your friend. I am your friend, so listen to me! Put a dot by it, and go on to the next question.

Repeat this process throughout your testing session. I do not care if you have 30 dots when you finish. Big deal. You have accomplished something significant: You have worked your way through the entire test. You know every question and concept they have to throw at you. You've seen it all. The pressure is off.

Here is what I want you to do when you finish going through the test this first time. Close your book. Get up. Go to the restroom. Shake out the tenseness in your muscles. Get a drink of water. Walk around for a minute or two to clear your head and relax. It will be time well spent to rid your body and mind of tension and stress and to loosen up. Then, before you go back in, stop and say out loud to use your auditory sense, "Thank goodness I have made it through this test *the first time.* Now I am going back in there to *finish acing this baby!*" Do not ignore what I am saying. It is important that your subconscious *hear* you affirm that you are going to pass this test. Repeat it over and over, out loud and silently. It is all a part of winning the mind game.

When you go back into the testing room, only return to the questions where you have dots. Remember, when anxiety goes down, productivity goes up. Because of that, you will be pleasantly surprised to see how many questions you will be able to answer quickly this time simply due to four reasons:

• The pressure is off. You have already seen everything on the test. There is nothing scary left. Psychologically, your subconscious has begun to relax; thus, your productivity will go up.

• You know that, in this instance, you do not have to make 100 on the TExES exam to pass it. Schools do not really care what your score is. They only care if you are certified. A passing score on TExES, plus other certification requirements, will accomplish that goal.

• There is something odd that happens after you have read the entire test. The *philosophy* as well as *key words and phrases* will settle into your subconscious and become familiar. If you have *not* spent too long pondering the difficult questions, generally the second time through, the appropriate answers will reveal themselves to you quickly. This is not as likely to happen if you have spent too long pondering each question when you read the question initially.

- You are no longer fighting the clock. You know you have already answered the ones that you are certain of. You do not have to stress over getting through the whole test the first time without running out of time. With this additional pressure off, your mind is freed to better comprehend what the more difficult questions are asking you.

If you do not have all the answers after your second time through, it is perfectly all right. Repeat the process. Close your book. Take a break, just like you did before. Your anxiety level should be *way* down by now because you know that you do not need to make 100. Just passing will do.

Regardless, keep repeating The Dot Game until you have answered all the questions. If that is over three times, guess on the ones you are not sure of and go home. This test is not the GRE. You are not penalized for wrong answers. It is unlikely you will have a divine intervention to tell you the right answers at this point. There is no sense in sitting there forever pondering a question that you are clueless about. Move on.

If you use The Dot Game, there is no way that you can run out of time. If you do *not* play The Dot Game, you will lose time and productivity on some questions, resulting in leaving a stack of easy questions unanswered. While you sit there stewing over Number 16, the clock is ticking away. Worse, your chances of getting Number 16 correct are going down because your anxiety level is going up. Do not do that. Just play The Dot Game as directed, and keep your forward progress moving.

There are some students who are simply slow readers or have difficulty with reading comprehension. This is often particularly true for test takers whose first language is not English. In these cases, The Dot Game is particularly beneficial. This test is long, has a lot of reading, and necessitates excellent comprehension skills. If you do not totally understand what is being asked, how can you expect to pick the right answer? Therefore, I strongly suggest that if you are a slow reader or if you have issues with reading comprehension that you check into getting some help right away. Don't wait till the week of the test when there is little that can be done. Try talking to a reading teacher for suggestions and then follow them. Another good idea is to take a reading comprehension or speed-reading course through community education, a local community college, or online. Regardless, it is *imperative* that you play The Dot Game to keep you moving and focused. You do not want to run out of time while you are still trying to figure out the second decision set.

Last, in the unlikely event that you have played The Dot Game two or three times and for whatever reason you suddenly fall into a coma until a test monitor comes to shake you awake and tell you it is time to leave, here is what you do: Guess. Guess like crazy, and do it quick before they throw you out. Then go seek medical attention about your coma.

This is very important: There are no correct answers left blank. You must put *something* down to have a *chance* of getting it right. Any chance beats no chance, so guess like crazy. You are not penalized for wrong answers. You do get credit for correct answers. If you get it right due to blind luck, congratulations. Pick the most ideal response to create the most ideal situation. Remember to forget reality and to think ideal. The developers of this test want to know if you know how to lead a school in an ideal manner. That is the goal behind every question. Therefore, forget how you have seen someone else respond to a similar situation in real life unless that person was performing in an ideal manner. The number one mistake people make on this test is to pick answers based on reality, things they have seen done in real life. Forget that. In response to every question ask yourself, "What is the most ideal response?" Once you have identified the most ideal response, you have the answer to the question even if it does sound Pollyanna-ish.

That, my friends, is how to play The Dot Game. It is deceptively simple. Play it and win. It will help you stay cool, calm, collected, confident, and almost downright cocky. More important, it will help you manage the clock and your stress and will help you ace this test the first time you take it!

THE DOG AND STAR GAME: A DECISION-MAKING STRATEGY

The principal TExES exam is a multiple choice test. You do not need to memorize facts. You *do* need to be able to synthesize and apply the philosophy of the nine competencies we discussed in Chapters 3 through 11 as well as the strategies presented here. There will be four answer choices. In the best of times, one of them will shout at you as being correct. That answer is a star. We like stars. They make our lives easy. Still, since you will be such a good test taker, you want to make sure you are right. Therefore, when you find a really good answer, otherwise known as a star, draw a little star by that response in your booklet. But keep reading. Do you see any more really good answers? If so, mark them too. By process of elimination, one of those stars has to be brighter than the other. That means, in truth, one is a star while another is a baby star, a twinkle. Think to yourself, if I can only pick one of these meteorites, which one will it be? Which one is the brightest? Which one has more language from the competencies in it? Which response includes the most Important Points to Remember as provided at the end of Chapters 3 through 11? That response is the star. Mark it.

While we love stars, there is another group of responses that we like just about as much. They are dogs. Dogs are *bad* answers. Why would we be watching for bad answers? Because there are only four response choices. If one of them is a dog, use those good old kinaesthetic and visual senses again and *draw a great big line through it.* As you progress through the test, you will take great pride in drawing *big, heavy lines* through those dogs. This is important for three reasons:

• Every time you identify a dog, your chances of getting the answer right go up by 25%.

• If you can find a dog *and* a puppy, mark both of them out. A puppy is another bad answer. It's just not quite as bad as the dog. But it is still wrong and you know it is wrong. By marking out both a dog and a puppy, you will increase your chances of getting the question right by 50%!

• It is good psychology for you to *feel and see* the results of this decision-making process. It adds to your subconscious confidence that you are attacking the test in a systematic and methodical manner, and that you are going to *pass* this test out of sheer diligence and conscientiousness. Therefore, be sure to draw a line through every answer you know is wrong. It's good psychology and helps you select the right answer.

Let's say that out of four potential choices, you did not find a star. However, as you are reading the responses, you find a twinkle, or a pretty good answer. You are not in love with it, but it will do. You also found a dog and a puppy. The other choice is just . . . there. There is not much for or against it. Or, as often happens, it is a perfectly good response. It just does not answer *this* question. They do that a lot. It tends to confuse people who think, "That is a good thing to do." Well, it may be. Just because a response says George Washington was the first president of the United States and you know that is true, does not mean it is the correct answer for this question. Beware! They love to throw in distracters like that, which are totally true. Do not let them trick you! If a response does not answer this question, it is a *wrong* response even if it is a good thing to do. Always bear in mind what *this question* is asking. That is why it is important to *underline key words or phrases in every question*. It helps to keep you focused on the *intent* of this question.

If you do not find a bright shining star, but you do find a twinkle, a puppy, a dog, and a non-issue, or distracter, your correct answer is the twinkle. It may not be an obvious meteorite like we love, but it will do. Mark it. It is the best choice available and will get the job done. We love stars, and we love dogs. We will settle for twinkles and puppies. Each time you can identify any of these, your chances of getting the question correct go up by 25%. If you can eliminate two, your chances go up by 50%. There will be many times when you can eliminate all three wrong choices. By process of elimination you now have the correct answer. Mega kudos!

MULTIPLE–MULTIPLES: TO MAXIMIZE SUCCESS, ALWAYS USE "THE PROCESS"

As we know, the entire test is multiple choice with four selections per problem. However, there are some questions that are more complex. They begin by presenting the question in the standard method. Next they list four potential solutions prefixed by roman numerals I, II, III, and IV. Beside those are the standard choices A, B, C, and D. The choices for A through D are various combinations of roman numerals I through IV.

These multiple-multiples drive some people crazy. I must admit that at one time I was against them. I felt they got away from the *intent* of the test, which is to determine entry-level skills for a new principal, and that they put undue focus on reading comprehension and test-taking skills. However, it is not up to me to write the test. This is the test as we have it today. We cannot change it, but we sure can pass it. We have the now-famous Elaine Wilmore Process. Memorize and practice The Process. It is about to become your new best friend.

Here is an example of how to use The Process. Stick with me here. We are going to do several examples to make sure you understand The Process.

Example: What is/are Dr. Wilmore's favorite thing(s) to eat?

   I. Raw minnows disguised as sushi

  II. Broccoli

 III. Italian food

 IV. Chocolate (YUMMY!)

A. I, II

B. II

C. I, II, III

D. IV

The above sample question requires you to know a little about my eating preferences. Here are some hints.

1. I do not eat raw fish of any kind. (Dog answer.)

2. I do like broccoli, but it is far from being my *favorite* food. (This would be a puppy response due to the key word being "favorite." In choosing answers be sure to look closely at every word. Your clue this time was "favorite.")

3. I have been to Italy four times and really, really like Italian food. (Twinkle response. Reading up to this point, it would be the best choice . . . but you keep reading to see *all* your options.)

4. Life is short. I can't live without chocolate. In times of high stress . . . chocolate. In times of celebration . . . chocolate. Needing a pick-me-up for the sheer pleasure of it . . . chocolate. There are no bad kinds of chocolate. All chocolate is good. The world revolves around chocolate. (Chocolate is a *star* answer! It takes nothing away from the Italian food. Italian food is still wonderful. By not selecting Italian food, we are not saying it isn't a good answer. It is just not the *best* answer. On the TExES exam, you

are looking for the *best* answer or the *brightest* star. In this instance, chocolate is outshining Italian food, although not by much.)

STEPS IN "THE PROCESS"

1. Do nothing until you are sure.

The first thing you will do on a "multiple-multiple" question is nothing until you are sure. So, after reading this question, you would look at the first, or I, response. It says, "Raw minnows disguised as sushi." Since you know I do not eat raw fish of any kind, you are *positive* (i.e., "sure") this could not possibly be my favorite food. Draw a line through Option I because we know it is not right. Since you are *sure*, you go to the *next step* in The Process. *That step* is not *reading the next response! Never skip steps! The key to The Process working so well is to follow it! Do not ever skip steps!*

2. Go straight to the bottom.

Since we are sure the first response is not the right answer, we now go straight to the A, B, C, D answers at the *bottom*.

- Look at Option A. Do we see a I in it? Yes, we do. Since there is a I in it and we are sure I is not the right answer, draw a line through all of Option A. It is a wrong response regardless of the rest of it. You have now improved your chances of getting this question correct by 25%. But we are not through.
- Look at Option B. Does it have a I in it? No, it does not. Since it does not have a I in it, we keep it. Don't draw a line through it.
- Look at Option C. Does it have a I in it? Yes, it does. Guess what we do. We draw a line through it because it cannot be the right answer. Now we have eliminated two of the possible answer choices while only having read item I. We have improved your chances of getting this question right by 50%.
- Look at Option D. Does it have a I in it? No, it does not, so we keep it. We know the answer will be either Option B or Option D.
- Move forward to the next step in The Process.

3. Compare and contrast the remaining options.

In our case, the remaining options are B and D. We do *not* immediately return to the top food choices. We compare and contrast the choices in B and D. Option B is broccoli. We think broccoli could be a decent answer, but we doubt it is my *favorite* food. Since we are not *sure* (see Step 1 of The Process), we take a look at Option D.

Option D is chocolate!!! We know I love chocolate! We also know it would be exceedingly unlikely for me to like broccoli more than chocolate. Since we have now compared and contrasted B and D and are *sure* about D, the correct answer is D.

At this point you may be asking yourself, what about Option C? In this case, it was totally irrelevant. It did not end up mattering that I do like Italian food a lot. It could just as well have said the sun comes up in the east. It's a "That's nice" response that simply does not matter because we followed The Process and did not skip steps!

Now, what would have happened if you had not followed The Process? If you had read all the options first instead of doing nothing till you are *sure*, the whole Italian thing would have confused you because you know I like it. But by following The Process *exactly*, you knew the Italian food had no relevance at all.

Let's try this same example again but show you other ways you can do it. What if the options were as follows?

A. I, IV

B. I, III

C. II

D. III, IV

By following The Process, we would still be *sure* Option I is a wrong answer. I have not suddenly developed a strong fondness for raw fish. By continuing to Step 2 of The Process we would go *straight to the bottom* where we would eliminate Options A and B because they both have an I in them. Remember, we would not have read choices III and IV *yet* to know I like them. We just know that since we are sure about I, that guarantees that both Options A and B are both wrong. *Draw a line through them.*

Next, we would proceed to Step 3, to compare and contrast the remaining options. In this case, those options would be C and D. By comparing and contrasting C and D, we quickly see they have nothing in common! This means that I either like II (broccoli) more than *both* Italian food and chocolate (highly unlikely) or vice versa. Now, let's be honest. We are all into health and fitness these days. But, come on. Who do you know that truthfully loves broccoli more than Italian food and chocolate? It's just not happening.

Therefore, based on comparing and contrasting Options C and D, we select D as the correct answer. Bingo! Another multiple-multiple bites the dust!

One last thing about the multiple-multiples: Sometimes the test developers are just plain kind to us. What if the choices had looked like this?

A. I, IV

B. I, III

C. I, II

D. III, IV

This one would make us all fall to our knees in gratitude. In Step 1 of The Process we would eliminate the whole sushi thing, choice I. In Step 2, we would go straight to the bottom where we would see, wonder of wonders, there is a I in Options A, B, and C! That means that, technically, without even reading Option D, by *process of elimination* we know it *must* be the answer! Upon reading Option D, we love it! It has both Italian food and chocolate! In other words, this one is just plain old *easy*. Believe it or not, there actually will be some questions on the test that are this obvious . . . if you are staying calm, cool, collected, confident, and almost downright cocky. If you are all stressed out, not following The Process, or ignoring The Dot Game after I told you over and over to use it to help you manage the clock and your anxiety, *you will not recognize these easy ones.* So, be alert, follow my suggestions, mark these easy ones, move one, and be happy. They are not trick questions. They are gifts.

Needless to say, many questions will not be this obvious. They will be less factual and will require application of decision making based on the 10 learner-centered leadership competencies. Still, you should *follow the same process.*

Multiple-multiples can turn out to be your best friend if you will follow this process. Students repeatedly tell me that by following this method they begin to wish *all* the questions on the test were multiple-multiples. Turn a potentially frightening situation into a positive one by following the fantastic Elaine Wilmore Process.

KEY WORDS AND THEMES: "SHERRYS" REVISITED

Review Chapters 3 through 11 on the learner-centered competencies. You do not need to memorize them. However, read them over and over, slowly, for comprehension and synthesis of their concepts. Think about what they mean. Practice visualizing how you will put them into practice when you pass this test and become a principal. Go back and review Chapter 2, "Standing on the Promises," particularly focusing on the discussion on important recurring concepts and themes as presented in Figure 2.2. You will see key words and concepts repeated such as multiple uses of data for a concept and *all* and *facilitate* as words. Sometimes you will even see answer choices that appear to almost *quote* a competency. When you see answer choices that utilize the same words or concepts, pick that answer. If the test developers had liked other concepts, language, or words better, they would have used them. Stick with ideas you *know* they like. That is why they are in the competencies!

THE IDEAL PRINCIPAL

Let's review the concept of the ideal principal. The ideal principal always does what is right, even when it is difficult or politically unpopular. Think "ideal," then mark the ideal response. Collaborate with everyone on everything. Facilitate and align all students, teachers, parents, and everyone else for maximum productivity and efficiency to ensure continuous student success. You are the ideal principal. You are on a relentless pursuit of excellence for all school and community stakeholders. If all else fails, think, "Which one of these crazy choices would Elaine put?" Then mark it because it *is the right answer!*

SUMMARY

The Dot Game is a strategy to help you utilize your time effectively while also keeping your anxiety level down and confidence up. Use it. Repeat it till you have completed the test. However, if you have gone through the test two to three times and still have dots left, mark the responses you think the ideal principal would do. Remember, this test is not designed for what the average, run-of-the-mill principal would do. It is built on a philosophy that all principals want to do the *right, moral,* and *ethical* things necessary to produce schools that maximize student learning, productivity, and character for an improved democratic society. Do *not* select answers that you think are what is actually done in schools if there is a *better* choice that reaches to a higher standard of moral or ethical responsibility to the school community.

By playing The Dot Game and The Dog and Star Game as well as always thinking "ideal," you will make good choices and pass the TExES exam ASAP. Once you pass it, get your certification, and land a great job leading a school, remember that it is your moral and ethical responsibility to do the right thing even when something else is easier. Live the competencies. Let your walk match your talk for the benefit of every student. We are not in leadership for a quick or easy fix. We are in it to have a real impact on our world, to leave a legacy of unparalleled excellence, and to know when we go to bed at night that we have done every single thing we can to make those things happen. There has never been a time in the past when you have been needed more. Go forth, and do well. I believe in you, so always remember me, how I have advised you, and, please, keep me updated on all the wonderful things you are going to accomplish.

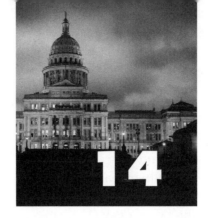

Creating a Personal Success Plan

Where There Is a Will, There Is a Way

You have goals of passing the TExES examination, obtaining principal certification, and becoming a great school leader focused on improving student performance. The first step in achieving these goals is passing this test. You have the necessary knowledge base from successful completion of your university or alternative preparation program. Upon reading, analyzing, and truly incorporating the concepts presented in this book into your leadership style, you will also have a solid understanding of the theoretical framework around which the test is constructed. The exam has been written to measure your understanding and capability of applying the nine principal learner-centered competencies fully detailed in Chapters 3 through 11. Section III has also provided you with specific strategies to help you make correct decisions regarding scenarios on the exam. What else can you do to assure you pass?

Two of Stephen Covey's *The 7 Habits of Highly Effective People* (1990) are

- begin with the end in mind, and
- sharpen the saw.

In preparing for what could possibly be the most important exam of your career, you need to do both. But, in simple language, what do these two habits mean, and how can you apply them in creating a personal plan for success on the principal TExES exam?

First, to begin with the end in mind means looking ahead to where you want to be (i.e., passing the TExES exam), then strategically calculating the exact things you must do between now and then to achieve it. Goals without deadlines are only dreams. Because of that, you must set a specific deadline for each thing you hope to accomplish in test preparation.

Waiting to the last minute will not get you where you want to be. You will either run out of time before the test or end up in such a frenzied state that it will be increasingly difficult to make prudent choices of answers to questions and data analysis.

Similarly, as you reflectively and insightfully consider the exact things you need to do while preparing for the exam, you also will be sharpening the saw. Covey (1990) gives the analogy of lumberjacks in a contest to see who can chop the most trees. One lumberjack immediately starts chopping. Another takes his time and spends several important minutes calmly sharpening the blade on his saw. Bystanders likely thought he had not picked a fine time to take up saw sharpening.

However, once this lumberjack was convinced his blade was ready, he began to saw on a tree. Because his saw was sharper than the other fellow's, he was more efficient and effective cutting down the trees. He subsequently won the contest. The point is once we look ahead to what we need to accomplish before the exam, once we begin now (our test preparation planning process) with the end in mind (actually passing the exam), we must also analyze, procure, and implement the best tools and resources available to help us sharpen our saws to maximize their utilization.

Taking these things into consideration, stop now and seriously consider the following. Aside from my principal preparation program and this wonderful book:

- What other exact resources would be beneficial in helping you understand and best be able to apply the nine principal competencies?
- Who can you talk to, or consult with? Who has the knowledge, expertise, and wisdom to best help you understand and be able to apply the competencies in scenario-based problem solving?
- Who can you talk to, or consult with, who can share helpful organizational techniques that can benefit you in the data analysis section of the exam?
- Who can you talk to, or consult with, to help you with time and stress management as you prepare for the test?
- Who can you talk to, or consult with, to help you create and implement your own personal success plan?
- Once developed and implemented, what modification and accountability mechanisms can you use to enhance the plan and hold you responsible for following it?

Each of these is a serious question. There are no absolutely right or wrong answers. They will vary from test taker to test taker and situation to situation. Figure 14.1 shows a sample template to help you organize your planning process. Whether you use it, or something different, just make sure you use something. Write it down. Include a timeline and accountability system. Remember, in the end, wanting to pass the TExES exam is only a dream if you do not have a plan with a responsible timeline and accountability process.

Figure 14.1 Personal Success Template

Idea or Project to Address	Resources I Will Need for	Projected Beginning Date	Projected Completion Date	Evaluation: How will I be able to measure what I have learned?	Accountability: How will I be held accountable?

TIPS FOR THOSE WHO HAVE NOT BEEN SUCCESSFUL ON THE EXAM . . . YET

For various reasons, sometimes a person will not immediately pass the test. Health, family, and stress issues are some reasons people do not pass. Because the test is long and involves a lot of reading, test takers who are slow readers, or who have poor are reading comprehension skills, sometimes have difficulty. But the major reason people do not immediately pass is a lack of proper understanding of the nine learner-centered competencies. If you fall in any of these categories, do not be discouraged. This is the longest and most reading-intensive TExES exam that currently exists. Developing and using a personal success plan such as the template provided in Figure 14.1 helps you to create a concrete schema to help you succeed. Thus, the real issue becomes identifying the specific things you can do to improve your scores. If you did not do well last time, study your scores. Is there a domain in which you came very close to passing? If so, what are the things you can do to focus and improve in this area? The same is true for your lowest domain. Really focus on this area because it is dragging you down. Your lowest domain is your highest area of need. If you do not have much time to prepare, concentrate your attention on the chapters of this book that address your lowest area. Seek solid ways to increase your knowledge base and application skills in this area. Do not be afraid to ask school administrators to help you. Most of them will want to help you, but they need guidance on how to do it. If you can share with them your greatest areas of need, they can center their mentoring efforts in those areas.

THE "ELAINE WILMORE 5-C PLAN"

If you have truly studied, synthesized, and internalized the leadership concepts presented in this book, created and utilized a personal success plan, and sought assistance and mentoring in targeted areas from people you respect, you should do quite well this time. However, there are some additional things you can do to improve both your likelihood and confidence. You need the benefit of the "Elaine Wilmore 5-C Plan." The 5-C Plan consists of going into this test

calm,

cool,

collected,

confident, and almost downright . . .

cocky.

I have had *numerous* people from around the state say that prior to attending my preparation seminars or reading my books, they had been unsuccessful in passing the principal or principal TExES exam. Yet after *doing what I have stressed to them to do,* they passed their test. Hearing this kind of news never fails to make me happy. Actually, this kind of news, particularly from someone who had yet to be successful on one of the tests, really makes me smile from the inside out. Like everyone else, I am human. I get tired (real tired, actually), and even I can get worn down from the stress of life. Hearing from people who pass the test, hearing the joy in their voices, cards, letters, and e-mails lifts me up more than you can ever know. Your success is important to me. I want you to pass this test. I want you to become the best principals our state and others have ever seen. Our kids deserve nothing less. Therefore, we have got to work together to get you through this test!

Here are some specific suggestions to help you do exactly that:

- Application of Competencies: Go back to each of the nine learner-centered competencies. Read, study, and analyze them slowly for comprehension, not memorization, of the concepts they represent.

- Remember, the key here is *comprehension* of the concepts, not memorizing them.

Figure 14.2   Utilize the "Elaine Wilmore 5-C Plan"

- To help you comprehend and be able to apply their *meaning*, develop a portfolio with nine sections. There should be one section for each of the nine competencies. Begin watching school-level administrators around you in various contexts. In your mind, try to associate every positive thing they do with at least one of the competencies. Take notes, collect artefacts, and write brief reflective summaries of each activity. Place the notes into the appropriate section of your competency portfolio. There is something about framing thoughts into logical sentences that helps us more fully understand what they mean. Otherwise, what could we write down? Writing the brief summaries will thus help you analyze the activity you have observed into its various components.

- Sometimes you will have difficulty deciding if an activity belongs with one or a different competency. That is all right. It probably does go both places. Do not stress over this. The principal's job is an integrated position. We are not going to split hairs over what goes where. You will not receive bonus points for knowing exactly which questions go with which competencies. *The important thing is that you are connecting real-life applications with the concepts of the competencies.* You are thus making the competencies come alive. You are internalizing and synthesizing them. When you see scenarios of principal behavior in the TExES questions or the data analysis section, you will already be accustomed to analyzing behaviors and making prudent organizational decisions. Your portfolio will help you select the appropriate responses. Your portfolio will be personal, authentic, and applied TExES preparation.

If you have taken the test before and not yet passed it look at your:

- *Content Analysis:* Analyze the score sheet or sheets you have received in previous TExES endeavors. Write down your scores *per domain* rather than your total score. Forget your total score. If you bring up your domain and competency scores, your domain and competency scores will automatically bring up your overall score.

- *Personal Strengths and Weaknesses:* Within your scores, you will have relative strengths, which are your higher scores. You will also have relative weaknesses, which are your lower scores. Target the areas you would like to focus on for this test administration. Go back to your college textbooks and notes for those areas. Review them. Study particularly the corresponding chapters of this book that go with those competencies. Study the additional resources that I have suggested *per competency*. In this way, your preparation will be focused on *your* greatest needs. You will be working *smarter* rather than harder.

- *Reading Comprehension or Speed Reading Courses/Review:* I am convinced there are many highly intelligent people who have had difficulty passing various TExES exams due to a combination of factors. Some are not prepared cognitively. They do not have the appropriate knowledge base. Others have, amazingly, never had the *philosophy* of learner-centered leadership stressed to them. How can anyone be expected to pass a test if they do not have a comprehension of the theoretical framework on which it is built? Others are lacking in language and test-taking skills. Test takers whose primary language is not English sometimes have to work harder to ensure they understand the intent of the questions and responses.

Having someone with whom to do these activities collaboratively will multiply the benefits for both you and him or her. If you have an encouraging mentor, supportive friend, or even a friendly classmate, ask them if once a week they will take the time to sit down and let you walk through your portfolio with them. It will be particularly beneficial if your partner is preparing for the test too. You can share your ideas, thoughts, and portfolios with each other, which will multiply the rewards. Orally describe each artefact, set of notes, and so forth, and then summarize how they apply to this competency and what you learned from them. The act of orally describing what something is and why you selected it will manifest itself in critical and reflective thinking. These are, of course, higher order thinking skills, which is exactly what this test is all about. Benjamin Bloom would be proud. So will you when you get your passing TExES scores!

Some, though, have difficulty with TExES due to the immense amount of reading involved. Every decision set and question involves reading, comprehension, analysis, and synthesis for application. Although many of these people are smart and successful in life, reading comprehension is not high on their talent lists. Sometimes comprehension is not the only problem. Sometimes they read very slowly. Some are also slowed down because English is not their first language. It takes time to read in English, process and possibly translate what has been read into their primary language, then convert everything back to English to pick a correct response. All of this takes time and time is not your friend. *I am your friend!* Do what I tell you to do! If you don't play the game my way, the clock could win instead of you. Once you start having to fight the clock, you're in trouble. Eventually, you may begin to panic. *We know for a fact that panic is counterproductive in passing the TExES exam and virtually any other high-stakes test.* When anxiety goes up, productivity goes down. That is not what we want. We want productivity to stay up and anxiety to stay down. Practice deep breathing or yoga relaxation techniques. I've never learned yoga, but I delivered three large babies by natural childbirth, thanks to the help of Lamaze breathing techniques. Believe me; those same Lamaze breathing techniques have served me quite well through the years when I have been stressed. In short, do whatever works to keep you calm as long as it is legal and moral.

If reading comprehension or speed is an issue with you, you already know it. There are various places, including Sylvan Learning Centers and university or school district continuing education courses that offer classes in these areas. Another good resource would be local English, language arts, or reading teachers. They often know of many good books, tapes, or techniques that would be beneficial. Your public library, as well as school and university libraries, also have resources to assist you. I cannot stress enough the importance of reading comprehension in passing this test. If you think you read well, but have been unsuccessful in passing the TExES exam more than once, what on earth do you stand to lose by seeking to improve your reading skills? Not only will it help you pass this test, it will also improve your quality of life in countless other areas.

TIPS FOR OUT-OF-STATE FUTURE TEXAS PRINCIPALS

Very often, there are people from out of state, particularly practicing administrators, who seek to become principals in the Great State of Texas. Welcome! We love our strong, independent state and welcome you to it. Be sure you bring along a firm commitment to learner-centered leadership and to improving student performance because that's what education in Texas is all about.

The competency information provided in this book will bring things you have known for years to the forefront of your mind. To my surprise, many of the states adjacent to Texas are not stressing learner-centered leadership. Or it could be that they are, but you have been out of school for a long time and not actively involved in this type of professional development. We can solve that.

It is particularly important for you to think "ideal principal." In many ways, it is more important for you than it is for the nonprincipals taking the test. Remember, this test is designed for *entry-level* administrative skills. If you have years of experience, you will have a tendency to look at potential responses from an experienced perspective. You know what will or will not work in real life.

Forget real life. Think *ideal.* If a response may seem a little *unrealistic* to you, but you know that in an *ideal school* with an *ideal principal* that is likely what would happen, *mark that answer!* It is the right one! The idea here is to lift the benchmark of principal behavior as much as possible, especially with new principals, to the level of ideal. Remember our pal Les Brown again. Aim for the moon. Even if you miss it, you will land among the stars. We want *every* principal, new and experienced, to aim for the moon, the very epitome of the ideal principal, every day in every way. In so doing, our schools may not reach the top, but they sure will achieve higher than they currently are. What on earth could be wrong with that?

The last thing I suggest is for you to get on the Internet and study different Academic Excellence Indicator System (AEIS) and Adequate Yearly Progress (AYP) reports for various districts and schools. Since AEIS reports are a Texas thing, you may not be familiar with their layout. But you will be familiar with the types of data presented therein. Look up an AEIS report, and play with it. Assess them for the good, the bad, and the ugly. Design interventions that could potentially improve student learning. Becoming familiar and comfortable with AEIS and AYP reports prior to testing will save you time and anxiety on the day you test. You will be able to whiz right through it, playing The Dot Game, of course. Remember: *Think ideal.*

EVERYONE—TEXANS AND NON-TEXANS ALIKE

What else should you do to prepare yourself cognitively, psychologically, and emotionally?

Mantras

The administrative TExES exams are mind games based on implementing student-centered leadership. The domains and competencies develop and portray this philosophy. In this book, you have studied, processed, and applied them in every conceivable scenario. Cognitively you are prepared. Logically, you should and will pass the test.

What about illogically? What if you are so frightened that you cannot think straight? What if, deep down, you are truly scared you will fail the test? What if your job or future job depends on passing? You cannot think about being an ideal principal or developing an ideal school because you are too busy breaking out in hives.

You've got to break that paradigm. Your mind is the front wheel of the wheelbarrow that drives your life. Your mind must be convinced you will not just pass TExES, you will ace it. You will knock it dead. You will do so well that they will audit your results. You will do great! You will make me proud! Frankly, you will simply be amazing! People will look at you in awe!

To convince your inner self of that, begin at this moment saying out loud, "I am going to ace this test. I am going to do great. I am thinking 'ideal' all day long." Do this a hundred times a day from now until you pass. Write it on 50 Post-it Notes and put them everywhere. Each time you see one, read it out loud. Say it with spirit. Practice being calm, cool, collected, confident, and almost downright cocky! Repeat the mantra until you, and everyone around you, is sick of hearing it. Repeat it alone, in public, in boring meetings, in your car, while exercising, or shopping. Sing it in the shower really loud. Repeat it until you drive yourself and others crazy. Repeat it over and over as you get ready and drive to the test. Keep repeating it as you take the test. You are what you believe you are. You are a success. You are going to make a real difference in this world. Believe it. Do it. You will be great!

THOSE TESTING ON A COMPUTER

All of the test-taking strategies described in Chapter 13 can be adapted to use on a computerized test. Whereas you cannot actually draw a line through answers you are certain are wrong, or put a star by those you are pretty certain are correct, you can modify and adjust. You will be given blank paper. When you are uncertain of an answer, or working The Process for multiple-multiples, do not copy the questions onto your scratch paper. However, do write down how they are set up. For example, for #15, you could write:

A.

B.

C.

D.

Or, for a *multiple-multiple* you could simply write:

I.

II.

III.

IV.

A. I, III

B. II, IV

C. II

D. I, II, III

Then work "The Process."

With this technique, you can cross things out or put stars by them just like the people who are taking the traditional paper-and-pencil test. For visual and kinaesthetic learners, writing things out is a tremendous testing asset.

FROM NOW TILL THE WEEK YOU TEST

From now till the test, review Section II of this book regularly. Put that in your personal success plan. Study the competencies. Read through them slowly as you focus on the concepts they represent. Do not attempt to memorize anything, but do focus on the terms, language, and common themes that emerge. Once a week, review Chapters 3 through 11. I do *not* want you to think, "Well, I read the book, so I am ready for the test." That is real nice, and you may pass the test. But you also need to prepare, integrate, synthesize, apply, and *not forget* all I have been preaching to you about these competencies.

By synthesizing the competencies over and over until you are sick of them and never want to see them again, you will become as familiar and comfortable with them and the concepts they represent as you currently are with driving to school. Driving to school may not be a big deal to you because you do it every day. But remember when you were first learning to drive? Driving *anywhere* was a big deal. You watched every corner, every traffic light, and likely gripped the steering wheel tightly when other cars came your way.

Think of these competencies as learning to drive. I want you so thoroughly familiar and comfortable with them that when you take the TExES, they will seem as natural as driving to school. You are the driver of this test. Drive it well.

THE WEEK YOU TEST

You have faithfully prepared. You have read Section II at least once a week until the week of the test. It is now time to get more intense. Reread the entire book. Focus this time on Section III with its strategies and techniques for success. Then *each night* before you go to bed, read through the competencies *again.* Do it as the last thing before you turn off the lights. Research says the last thing you have on your mind before falling asleep stays in your mind all night long. That is exactly where we want this information to be. We want it working its way through your mind while you sleep, eat, work, bathe, or fall into a coma.

As before, read for comprehension, not memorization. By reading the competencies many times, key words and phrases that appear on the test, especially in answers, will jump right out at you as if they were in bold print. That is good. Those are *stars*. Mark them. We know if the test developers had liked other words or phrases better, they would have used them. When they use their own language, they are *giving* you the answer. Take them up on it and say, "Oh! Thank you!"

Then send me chocolate, plain with no nuts, as a thank-you for clueing you in on all this. I don't like nuts in my chocolate because we already have way too many nuts in education. I also really like pink roses, just in case you wanted to know. There are no nuts in roses.

WHAT TO DO, AND NOT DO, THE NIGHT BEFORE THE TEST

The night before the test is similar to the last minutes of the test if you are still sitting there. If you are not familiar with the competencies and test-taking strategies presented here by that point, it is not going to come to you by osmosis or divine intervention. However, I have had more than one student promise me that prayer works. I am a big believer in prayer myself.

I pray for all my students before they test. From this point on, consider yourself my student.

In truth, this is what I want you to do. You will test on a Saturday. On the Friday before you test, come home from school or wherever and *relax.* Go out to dinner. Take in a movie that is *light* and fun with pure, mindless drivel. Do *not* go see anything stressful. You have enough stress in your life right now. You can see intense or stressful movies after the test when you are so relieved to have it behind you that you know that you could single-handedly slay dragons. Think of it as a victory march.

But the night before the test, you want mindless drivel. You want *absolutely nothing stressful* going on. Talk to your family, assuming you have one, ahead of time. Make sure they understand the *importance* of you having a calm night. If the cat has kittens, let someone else tend to it. As far as I am concerned, I do not even want you to *know about it.* And if you win the Publisher's Clearinghouse, don't let anyone tell you until *after* this blasted test. Otherwise, it would be a distraction for you to think about how you are going to spend, invest, or give away all that money. After the test, you can celebrate and, of course, invite me.

On the night before the test, relax. Go out to dinner some place you like. Do something fun. Come home early. Take a nice, hot bubble bath, preferably with *peach* bubbles, in my honor, of course. Men, just take the bubble bath, and hush up. Your wives will love it! You will become very relaxed, which is exactly the point.

Then go to bed. You may read through the competencies one last time. If you do not know them by now, cramming will not help. Read through them, turn off the lights, and say your prayers. The party is over.

WHAT TO DO, AND NOT DO, THE MORNING OF THE TEST

Set your clock to get up in plenty of time, particularly if you are assigned a morning testing. I do not want you rushed and messing up all that good relaxation from last night. Have *plenty of time* to get ready and arrive. If necessary, get directions and practice driving the route to the testing site. Don't be late!

Eat something. Even if you are not a breakfast person, eat something anyway. Research shows people who have something in their stomachs to fuel their bodies perform better. We want you to have *peak performance.* This is Olympics Day for you. Don't you know all those athletes have specially designed meals to ensure peak performance? This is your Olympics. You may not have a nutritionist at your house, but you do have something loaded with protein. Avoid carbohydrates this morning. They may give you a quick rush, but by midmorning, your blood sugar will crash. Testing day is not the day for your blood sugar to crash. Eat protein instead. After the test, you can pig out on as many carbs as you want but not now!

Dress comfortably and in layers. This may be the only time in your life that looking good does not count. Wear something comfortable. This includes your shoes. You do not need aching feet during the TExES examination. If you decide your feet hurt during the test, shed the shoes. If your feet tend to get cold when you are nervous, bring extra socks. Dress in layers. I have had *multiple* students around the entire state complain that the testing sites are really cold. If you dress in layers, you can shed some of them if you get too warm. There is nothing worse than being cold during a test. From the other perspective, some people respond to stress by getting really hot and sweating. Others respond by their blood pressure slowing down instead of going up. They get cold. By dressing in layers, you will be prepared for any situation. And, last, if you have a lucky charm or talisman, wear it.

Arrive at the test site early. You do not want to be rushed or to take any chances with traffic, wrecks, emergencies, nuclear attack, and so on. There will be a large number of other test takers at your testing site. Most of them will *not* be taking the same test as you. The lengths of different tests vary, so do not be surprised or chagrined if people sitting around you get up and leave before you are anywhere close to being through. Do not assume that they are innately brilliant and that you are a bump on a pickle. That is not true. *You* are the one that is innately brilliant and *fabulously* well prepared. They may be taking a different test. Or they have guessed their way all the way through our test and are hoping for a computer miracle during grading. *You* stay focused on taking care of your own business. Do not worry about theirs.

Make sure you remember to play The Dot Game. It is such a simple strategy that you may be tempted to not do it. Do it anyway. It will save you both time and grief. It is a very very good test-taking strategy to maximize your productivity. Both your body and your mind need this structure for addressing confusing questions. Review everything about The Dot Game the week of the test. Apply what you know. It is a well-seasoned game and has greater validity than the lottery. Utilize the Dog and Star Game. Work your way through the test two to three times using both strategies. Then hang it up. Remember, you do not have to make 100% on this test. All you have to do is pass it. Speaking as someone who has spent nine glorious years serving on a public school board, I can assure you that boards do not utilize TExES exam scores when selecting school administrators. You are well prepared for this test. You have answered every question. You have given it your all. You are done. Go home!

LIVING YOUR LIFE AFTER THE TEST

Celebrate!!!! Although most people think that they leave the testing site brain dead simply due to the length of the test, you will also know in your heart that you passed this test. You will have a deep sense of accomplishment. You will feel an even greater sense of accomplishment the day you get your scores. But, until then, there is not one more thing you can do except celebrate. You deserve it. If you want to see an action thriller tonight, go do it. If you want to run the Boston Marathon, go do it. If you want to eat your weight in chocolate, invite me. But whatever you do, do it because it is something that fills your soul with joy. You have accomplished a major goal. You have taken and passed the principal TExES exam. You may not have your scores yet, but you know something that the computer does not. *You won!*

Go forth and make every day of your life all it can be for yourself and others. Do something kind for a stranger. Make a difference in the life of at least one person every day. Change the world, one school at a time. Yes, I do realize that this sounds like a Pollyanna way to approach life and educational leadership. But our world has enough negativity and ugliness in it. We have terrorists, wars, poverty, hunger, abuse, disease, lack of respect for others with different opinions and perspectives; the list goes on and on. We are surrounded by it.

Let's be different. Let's do everything we can to fill the world with joy. Idealistic? Yes. Impossible? No, not if you will help me.

Will you come along?

SECTION IV

After You Pass the Test

That's What It's All About!

15

That's What It's All About

Actually Becoming Certified

Once you receive your passing scores in the mail, you can shout for joy, jump up and down, call your entire family and friends, toss young children in the air, shout the news to strangers on the street, *send me roses and chocolate*, and be quite proud of yourself. You have accomplished a very great thing! I can already tell you just how proud I am of you. Now, don't let me down! You must go out there and be the ideal principal that you have proven that you know how to be. I am counting on you to do exactly that.

Figure 15.1 First One, Now the Other!

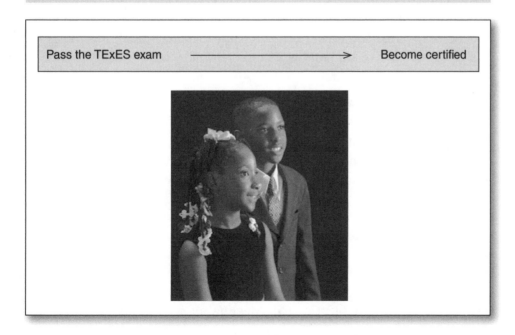

Pass the TExES exam ⟶ Become certified

However, after the celebrating, there are a few things left for you to do to actually obtain your principal certification. It is your responsibility to officially apply for your certificate with the State Board for Educator Certification (SBEC) at www.sbec.state.tx.us. There will be a certification fee, which you will pay directly to them.

Your university, or alternative preparation program, will already have received your scores from the State. *After* you have gone to the SBEC website, applied for your certificate, and paid your fee, you should contact the certification office at your university or alternative preparation program. Their verification and endorsement of your application is required. However, they cannot go online to approve your application if you have not applied for it. That's why you must do the online application through SBEC *before* contacting your certification officer. Do not forget the order of these important steps. Without doing them, you will not become certified regardless of how many tests you ace. Many, but not all, universities and alternative programs will charge you a small processing fee for completing your certification paperwork. To avoid confusion, remember that this is a different fee from the one you paid SBEC for your actual certification.

If you are an out-of-state test taker and not directly affiliated with any Texas university or approved alternative provider, you will need to contact SBEC directly regarding your certification paperwork.

During the time that it takes SBEC to process your paperwork, you are not yet officially certified. However, you are *certifiable*. This means you *are* eligible to be employed as a certified principal. The school district may require you to present evidence that you have completed all program requirements including passing your TExES exam. This is something your university will be pleased to provide. Usually, a simple letter on official university (or alternative program) letterhead stating your status will suffice. Certifications are now provided online so both you and your school can see when your actual certification is finalized. It is a wonderful thing when you see your certification appear by your name online. Print it out, and show it off to everyone you see. Tell them how hard you worked to get that piece of paper and how much you *really* love me for helping you get it. It's your job to make me famous, but that won't be on the TExES exam.

KNOCK THE TOP OUT OF IT!

With today's critical shortage of certified administrators, you could very well be hired as a principal before your certification becomes official. In fact, it is entirely possible that you could be hired before you even take the test. Regardless, you still must take the test. Having the job before you are certified does not exempt you from taking and passing the TExES exam. If that happens to you, do not blow off the test. It is still very serious to your career. Make sure you still study, prepare, and do every single thing I have told you to do to pass this test.

In the end, certification is more than a necessary step to your long-term employment as a school principal. Meeting all certification requirements through course work, practicums or internships, and the TExES examination are all designed for one purpose. *That purpose is to help you be the best principal on the face of this earth.* Nothing less will do. Is it a competition to be the best principal? Of course it's not. We want each and every school to be absolutely outstanding. We want every teacher to be able to teach where each student can and will learn. We want every student to graduate equipped for success in life regardless if that means entering the world of work, the military, or higher education. We want every graduate to be an informed, voting citizen within a literate, free, and democratic society.

Until all of this happens, we are not through with our work. We have not reached our destination where all schools and all of society are ideal. Early in this book, I told you that I am the Pollyanna of school leadership. I reminded you that we already have enough educational cynics and do not need any more. Stretching toward the ideal may, or may not, be realistic. But it is absolutely necessary that you aim for it. If we don't aim for ideal, how will we ever make significant strides toward reaching it? Your part in this is to be the best principal your school, town, the Great State of Texas, and the world have ever seen. That is what it will take to change, to improve, and to enhance our global society, one school at a time. Let's start now with you.

Will it be a daunting task? Yes, it will. Will you become tired, frustrated, and totally disgusted with complicated, complex community, school, state, and federal politics? Yes, at times you will. But will this also be the most challenging and personally rewarding job you could ever imagine? Without a doubt it will be. There will be tears of fatigue and frustration, but there will also be tears of joy and elation. There will be times you want to beat your head against a wall or prefer to beat a few other people's heads instead. Yet there will also be times of jumping up and down internally and externally over something magnificent that has happened, something that those with lesser faith believed could not be done. Yet you knew that it could. They were the cynics while you were the idealist. You knew that good things *would* happen because there is nothing on this earth that can make you give up in your continuing quest to change the world one school at a time.

You have now passed the TExES examination and are headed into your future with anticipation, hope, joy, courage, perseverance, and a little bit of fear. May every day of your journey to do what is right, to do what is ideal, to stay proactive, positive, and persuasive, be the best day imaginable. It is all before you now. Just reach out and take it. You've worked for it. You've earned it. It's yours. Just remember to send me the chocolate and roses.

May you be forever blessed. Go forth, and make me proud. Make the world a better place. Together we *can* be the difference. Will you join me as we try?

Now, let's do it! Go knock the top out of this test!

Your friend and mentor now and forever,

Elaine L. Wilmore, Ph.D.

Eternally grateful to be the daughter of my parents,
the late Lee and Irene Litchfield of Port Arthur, Texas

References

Covey, S. R. (1990). *The 7 habits of highly effective people.* New York, NY: Simon & Schuster.

Maslow, A. H. (1970). *Motivation and personality.* New York, NY: Harper & Row.

Texas Education Agency. (2006). *Texas Examinations of Educator Standards: Preparation manual: Principal. 068.* Austin, TX: Author. Retrieved November 3, 2012, from http://www.texes.ets.org/assets/pdf/testprep_manuals/068_principal_82762_web.pdf

Wilmore, E. L. (2007). *Teacher leadership: Improving teaching and learning from inside the classroom.* Thousand Oaks, CA: Corwin.

Suggested Additional Reading

This list is not intended to be an exhaustive guide but rather a source for supplemental reading that supports the concepts presented in the Principal TExES Exam. Many of these resources include content that is relevant to more than one domain.

DOMAIN I: SCHOOL COMMUNITY LEADERSHIP

Abrams, J. (2009). *Having hard conversations.* Thousand Oaks, CA: Corwin.

Bates, D., Durka, G., & Schweitzer, F. (2006). *Education, religion and society: Essays in honour of John M. Hull.* New York, NY: Routledge.

Beaudoin, M. N., & Taylor, M. (2004). *Creating a positive school culture: How principals and teachers can solve problems together.* Thousand Oaks, CA: Corwin.

Bell, L., & Stevenson, H. (2006). *Education policy: Process, themes and impact.* New York, NY: Routledge.

Bennis, W. (1989). *Why leaders can't lead.* San Francisco, CA: Jossey-Bass.

BenShea, N. (2000). *What every principal would like to say . . . and what to say next time.* Thousand Oaks, CA: Corwin.

Blair-Stanford, N., & Dickmann, M. H. (2002). *Connecting leadership to the brain.* Thousand Oaks, CA: Corwin.

Blanchard, K., & Bowles, S. (1998). *Gung-ho!* New York, NY: William Morrow.

Blanchard, K., Oncken, W., Jr., & Burrows, H. (1989). *The one minute manager meets the monkey.* New York, NY: William Morrow.

Blanchard, K., & Peale, N. V. (1988). *The power of ethical management.* New York, NY: William Morrow.

Blanchard, K., Zigarmi, P., & Zigmari, D. (1985). *Leadership and the one minute manager.* New York, NY: William Morrow.

Blankstein, A. M., & Houston, P. D. (2011). *Leadership for social justice and democracy in our schools.* Thousand Oaks, CA: Corwin.

Bolman, L. G., & Deal, T. E. (2001). *Leading with soul: An uncommon journey of spirit.* San Francisco, CA: Jossey-Bass.

Bolman, L. G., & Deal, T. E. (2002). *Reframing the path to school leadership: A guide for teachers and principals.* Thousand Oaks, CA: Corwin.

Brock, B. L., & Grady, M. L. (2000). *Rekindling the flame.* Thousand Oaks, CA: Corwin.

Brower, R. E., & Balch, B. V. (2005). *Transformational leadership & decision making in schools.* Thousand Oaks, CA: Corwin.

Brubaker, D. L. (2006). *The charismatic leader: The presentation of self and the creation of educational settings.* Thousand Oaks, CA: Corwin.

Burke, M. A., & Picus, L. O. (2001). *Developing community-empowered schools.* Thousand Oaks, CA: Corwin.

Capasso, R. L., & Daresh, J. C. (2001). *The school administrator internship handbook: Leading, mentoring, and participating in the internship program.* Thousand Oaks, CA: Corwin.

Carter, S. C. (2010). *On purpose: How great school cultures form strong character.* Thousand Oaks, CA: Corwin.

Chadwick, K. G. (2004). *Improving schools through community engagement: A practical guide for educators.* Thousand Oaks, CA: Corwin.

Cherry, D., & Spiegel, J. (2006). *Leadership, myth, & metaphor: Finding common ground to guide effective school change.* Thousand Oaks, CA: Corwin.

Covey, S. R. (1990). *Principle-centered leadership.* New York, NY: Simon & Schuster.

Covey, S. R., Merrill, A. R., & Merrill, R. R. (1994). *First things first.* New York, NY: Simon & Schuster.

Daresh, J. C., & Lynch, J. (2010). *Improve learning by building community.* Thousand Oaks, CA: Corwin.

Datnow, A., & Murphy, J. F. (2002). *Leadership lessons from comprehensive school reforms.* Thousand Oaks, CA: Corwin.

Davies, B., & Brighouse, T. (2009). *Passionate leadership in education.* Thousand Oaks, CA: Corwin.

DePree, M. (1989). *Leadership is an art.* New York, NY: Dell.

DePree, M. (1997). *Leading without power: Finding hope in serving community.* San Francisco, CA: Jossey-Bass.

Duncan, S. F., & Goddard, H. W. (2005). *Family life education: Principles and practices for effective outreach.* Thousand Oaks, CA: Sage.

Dunklee, D. R. (2000). *If you want to lead, not just manage: A primer for principals.* Thousand Oaks, CA: Corwin.

Dunklee, D. R., & Shoop, R. J. (2001). *The principal's quick-reference guide to school law: Reducing liability, litigation, and other potential legal tangles.* Thousand Oaks, CA: Corwin.

Dyer, K. M. (2000). *The intuitive principal.* Thousand Oaks, CA: Corwin.

Earl, L. M., & Katz, S. (2006). *Leading schools in a data-rich world: Harnessing data for school improvement.* Thousand Oaks, CA: Corwin.

Eisner, E. W. (2005). *Reimagining schools: The selected works of Elliot W. Eisner.* New York, NY: Routledge.

Elias, M., Arnold, H., & Steiger Hussey, C. (Eds.). (2002). *EQ + IQ = best leadership practices for caring.* Thousand Oaks, CA: Corwin.

Epstein, J. L., Sanders, M. G., Sheldon, S. B., Simon, B. S., Salinas, K. C., Jansorn, N. R., et al. (2009). *School, family, and community partnerships: Your handbook for action* (3rd ed.). Thousand Oaks, CA: Corwin.

Erickson, C. L., Morley, R. E., & Veale, J. R. (2002). *Practical evaluations for collaborative services.* Thousand Oaks, CA: Corwin.

Feinberg, W. (2006). *For goodness sake: Religious schools and education for democratic citizenry.* New York, NY: Routledge.

Fiore, D. J., & Whitaker, T. (2001). *Dealing with difficult parents (and with parents in difficult situations).* Larchmont, NY: Eye on Education.

Fullan, M. (2001). *Leading in a culture of change.* San Francisco, CA: Jossey-Bass.

Fullan, M. (2005). *Leadership & sustainability: System thinkers in action.* Thousand Oaks, CA: Corwin.

Fullan, M. (2010). *The moral imperative realized.* Thousand Oaks, CA: Corwin.

Giancola, J. M., & Hutchinson, J. K. (2005). *Transforming the culture of school leadership: Humanizing our practice.* Thousand Oaks, CA: Corwin.

Glaser, J. (2005). *Leading through collaboration: Guiding groups to productive solutions.* Thousand Oaks, CA: Corwin.

Goldring, E., & Berends, M. (2009). *Leading with data: Pathways to improve your school.* Thousand Oaks, CA: Corwin.

Halstead, J. M., & Pike, M. (2006). *Citizenship and moral education: Values in action.* New York, NY: Routledge.

Hargreaves, A., & Shirley, D. (2009). *The fourth way: The inspiring future for educational change.* Thousand Oaks, CA: Corwin.

Harris, S. (2005). *Bravo teacher! Building relationships with actions that value others.* Larchmont, NY: Eye on Education.

Holcomb, E. L. (2001). *Asking the right questions: Techniques for collaboration and school change* (2nd ed.). Thousand Oaks, CA: Corwin.

Houston, P. D., & Sokolow, S. L. (2006). *The spiritual dimension of leadership: 8 key principles to leading more effectively.* Thousand Oaks, CA: Corwin.

Hoy, W. H., & Miskel, C. G. (2012). *Educational administration: Theory, research, and practice* (5th ed.). New York, NY: McGraw-Hill.

Hoyle, J. (2006). *Leadership and futuring: Making visions happen* (2nd ed.). Thousand Oaks, CA: Corwin.

Hoyle, J. R. (2002). *Leadership and the force of love: Six keys to motivating with love.* Thousand Oaks, CA: Corwin.

Israel, S. E., Sisk, D. A., & Block, C. C. (2006). *Collaborative literacy: Using gifted strategies to enrich learning for every student.* Thousand Oaks, CA: Corwin.

Jayanthi, M., & Nelson, J. S. (2001). *Savvy decision making: An administrator's guide to using focus groups in schools.* Thousand Oaks, CA: Corwin.

Johnson, S. (1998). *Who moved my cheese?* New York, NY: Putnam.

Johnston, G. L., Townsend, R. S., Gross, G. E., Lynch, P., Garcy, L. M., Roberts, B. B., et al. (2009). *The superintendent's planner: A monthly guide and reflective journal.* Thousand Oaks, CA: Corwin.

Josephson, M. S., & Hanson, W. (1998). *The power of character.* San Francisco, CA: Jossey-Bass.

Kaser, J., Mundry, S., Stiles, K. E., & Loucks-Horsley, S. (2006). *Leading every day: 124 actions for effective leadership.* Thousand Oaks, CA: Corwin.

Kilmek, K. J., Ritzenhein, E., & Sullivan, K. D. (2008). *Generative leadership: Shaping new futures for today's schools.* Thousand Oaks, CA: Corwin.

Kochanek, J. R. (2005). *Building trust for better schools: Research-based practices.* Thousand Oaks, CA: Corwin.

Kosmoski, G. J., & Pollack, D. R. (2000). *Managing difficult, frustrating, and hostile conversations: Strategies for savvy administrators.* Thousand Oaks, CA: Corwin.

Kouzes, J. M., & Posner, B. Z. (1998). *Encouraging the heart: A leader's guide to rewarding and recognizing others.* San Francisco, CA: Jossey-Bass.

Kowalski, T. J. (2006). *The school superintendent: Theory, practice, and cases.* Thousand Oaks, CA: Sage.

Krovetz, M. L. (2008). *Fostering resilience: Expecting all students to use their minds and hearts well* (2nd ed.). Thousand Oaks, CA: Corwin.

Krzyzewski, M., & Phillips, D. T. (2000). *Leading with the heart: Coach K's successful strategies for basketball, business, and life.* New York, NY: Warner Books.

Longworth, N. (2006). *Learning cities, learning regions, learning communities: Lifelong learning and local government.* New York, NY: Routledge.

Louis, K. S. (2005). *Organizing for school change.* New York, NY: Routledge.

Lovely, S. (2006). *Setting leadership priorities: What's necessary, what's nice, and what's got to go.* Thousand Oaks, CA: Corwin.

Maxwell, J. C. (1995). *Developing the leaders around you.* Nashville, TN: Thomas Nelson.

McEwan, E. K. (2004). *How to deal with parents who are angry, troubled, afraid, or just plain crazy* (2nd ed.) Thousand Oaks, CA: Corwin.

Miller, J. P. (2006). *Educating for wisdom and compassion: Creating conditions for timeless learning.* Thousand Oaks, CA: Corwin.

Olssen, M., Codd, J. A., & O'Neill, A. (2004). *Education policy: Globalization, citizenship, and democracy.* Thousand Oaks, CA: Sage.

Osier, J. L., & Fox, H. P. (2001). *Settle conflicts right now! A step-by-step guide for K–6 classrooms.* Thousand Oaks, CA: Corwin.

Osterman, K. F., & Kottkamp, R. B. (2004). *Reflective practice for educators: Professional development to improve student learning.* Thousand Oaks, CA: Corwin.

Pellicer, L. O. (2007). *Caring enough to lead* (2nd ed.). Thousand Oaks, CA: Corwin.

Peters, T., & Waterman, R. H. (1993). *In search of excellence.* New York, NY: Warner Bros.

Preble, B., & Gordon, R. (2011). *Transforming school climate and learning: Beyond bullying and compliance.* Thousand Oaks, CA: Corwin.

Pryor, B. W., & Pryor, C. R. (2005). *The school leader's guide to understanding attitude and influencing behavior: Working with teachers, parents, students, and the community.* Thousand Oaks, CA: Corwin.

Reagan, T. G., Case, C. W., & Brubacher, J. W. (2000). *Becoming a reflective educator: How to build a culture of inquiry in the schools.* Thousand Oaks, CA: Corwin.

Rebore, R. W., & Walmsley, A. L. E. (2009). *Genuine school leadership: Experience, reflection, and beliefs.* Thousand Oaks, CA: Corwin.

Reinhartz, J., & Beach, D. M. (2001). *Foundations of educational leadership: Changing schools, changing roles.* Boston, MA: Allyn & Bacon.

Roberts, S. M., & Pruitt, E. Z. (2003). *Schools as professional learning communities: Collaborative activities and strategies for professional development.* Thousand Oaks, CA: Corwin.

Rubin, H. (2002). *Collaborative leadership: Developing effective partnerships in communities and schools* (2nd ed.). Thousand Oaks, CA: Corwin.

Sagor, R., & Rickey, D. (2012). *The relentless pursuit of excellence: Lessons from a transformational leader.* Thousand Oaks, CA: Corwin.

Sanders, M. G. (2006). *Building school-community partnerships: Collaboration for student success.* Thousand Oaks, CA: Corwin.

Schumaker, D. R., & Sommers, W. A. (2001). *Being a successful principal: Riding the wave of change without drowning.* Thousand Oaks, CA: Corwin.

Seiler, T. L. (2001). *Developing your case for support.* San Francisco, CA: Jossey-Bass.

Sergiovanni, T. J. (2001). *The principalship: A reflective practice perspective* (4th ed.). Needham Heights, MA: Allyn & Bacon.

Sergiovanni, T. J. (2007). *Rethinking leadership: A collection of articles* (2nd ed.). Thousand Oaks, CA: Corwin.

Smith, M. L., Miller-Kahn, L., Heinecke, W., & Jarvis, P. F. (2003). *Political spectacle and the fate of American schools.* New York, NY: Routledge.

Sparks, D. (2006). *Leading for results: Transforming teaching, learning, and relationships in schools.* Thousand Oaks, CA: Corwin.

Spears, L., Lawrence, M., & Blanchard, K. (2002). *Focus on leadership: Servant-leadership for the 21st century.* New York, NY: Wiley & Sons.

Sperry, D. J. (1999). *Working in a legal and regulatory environment: A handbook for school leaders.* Larchmont, NY: Eye on Education.

Streshly, W. A., Walsh, J., & Frase, L. E. (2001). *Avoiding legal hassles: What school administrators really need to know* (2nd ed.). Thousand Oaks, CA: Corwin.

Strike, K. A. (2007). *Ethical leadership in schools: Creating community in an environment of accountability.* Thousand Oaks, CA: Corwin.

Sullivan, S., & Glanz, J. (2006). *Building effective learning communities: Strategies for leadership, learning, & collaboration.* Thousand Oaks, CA: Corwin.

Taulbert, C. L. (2006). *Eight habits of the heart for educators: Building strong school communities through timeless values.* Thousand Oaks, CA: Corwin.

Terrell, R. D., & Lindsey, R. B. (2009). *Culturally proficient leadership: The personal journey begins within.* Thousand Oaks, CA: Corwin.

Veale, J. R., Morley, R. E., & Erickson, C. L. (2001). *Practical evaluation for collaborative services: Goals, processes, tools, and reporting systems for school-based programs.* Thousand Oaks, CA: Corwin.

Weiss, H. B., Kreider, H., & Labez, M. E. (2005). *Preparing educators to involve families: From theory to practice.* Thousand Oaks, CA: Sage.

West, C. E., & Derrington, M. L. (2009). *Leadership teaming: The superintendent-principal relationship.* Thousand Oaks, CA: Corwin.

Whitaker, T. A., Whitaker, B., & Lumpa, D. (2000). *Motivating and inspiring teachers: The educational leader's guide for building staff morale.* Larchmont, NY: Eye on Education.

Williams, R. B. (2006). *More than 50 ways to build team consensus.* Thousand Oaks, CA: Corwin.

Wilmore, E. L. (2002). *Principal leadership: Applying the educational leadership constituent council (ELCC) standards.* Thousand Oaks, CA: Corwin.

Wilmore, E. L. (2008). *Superintendent leadership: Applying the educational leadership constituent council standards for improved district performance.* Thousand Oaks, CA: Corwin.

York-Barr, J., Sommers, W. A., Ghere, G. S., & Montie, J. (2006). *Reflective practice to improve schools: An action guide for educators.* Thousand Oaks, CA: Corwin.

DOMAIN II: INSTRUCTIONAL LEADERSHIP

Alford, B. J., & Nino, M. C. (2011). *Leading academic achievement for English language learners: A guide for principals.* Thousand Oaks, CA: Corwin.

Banks, J. (2006). *Race, culture, and education: The selected works of James A. Banks.* New York, NY: Routledge.

Banks, J. A., & Banks, C. M. (1996). *Multicultural education: Issues and perspectives.* Boston, MA: Allyn & Bacon.

Barker, C. L., & Searchwell, C. J. (2001). *Writing year-end teacher improvement plans—right now!!* Thousand Oaks, CA: Corwin.

Barth, R. S. (2003). *Lessons learned: Shaping relationships and the culture of the workplace.* Thousand Oaks, CA: Corwin.

Beach, D. M., & Reinhartz, J. (2000). *Supervisory leadership.* Boston, MA: Allyn & Bacon.

Bender, W. N. (2012). *Differentiating instruction for students with learning disabilities: New best practices for general and special educators.* Thousand Oaks, CA: Corwin.

BenShea, N. (2006). *The journey to greatness: And how to get there!* Thousand Oaks, CA: Corwin.

Bjork, L. G., & Kowalski, T. J. (Eds.). (2005). *The contemporary superintendent: Preparation, practice, and development.* Thousand Oaks, CA: Corwin.

Blanchard, K., & Johnson, S. (1981). *The one minute manager.* New York, NY: Berkley.

Blankenstein, A. M. (2013). *Failure is not an option: Six principles that guide student achievement in high-performing schools.* Thousand Oaks, CA: Corwin.

Bracey, G. W. (2000). *Bail me out! Handling difficult data and tough questions about public schools.* Thousand Oaks, CA: Corwin.

Brewer, E. W., DeJonge, J. O., & Stout, V. J. (2001). *Moving online: Making the transition from traditional instruction and communication strategies.* Thousand Oaks, CA: Corwin.

Brooks-Young, S. (2007). *Critical technology issues for school leaders.* Thousand Oaks, CA: Corwin.

Browne, J. R., II. (2012). *Walking the equity talk: A guide for culturally courageous leadership in school communities.* Thousand Oaks, CA: Corwin.

Bucher, R. D. (2000). *Diversity consciousness: Opening our minds to people, cultures, and opportunities.* Upper Saddle River, NJ: Prentice Hall.

Burrello, L. C., Lashley, C., & Beatty, E. E. (2001). *Educating all students together: How school leaders create unified systems.* Thousand Oaks, CA: Corwin.

Burton, V. R. (2000). *Rich minds, rich rewards.* Dallas, TX: Pearl.

Capper, C. A., & Frattura, E. M. (2009). *Meeting the needs of students of all abilities: How leaders go beyond inclusion* (2nd ed.). Thousand Oaks, CA: Corwin.

Carob, M. (2000). *What every principal should know about teaching reading.* Syosset, NY: National Reading Styles Institute.

Carr, J. F., & Harris, D. (2009). *Improve standards-based learning: A process guide for educational leaders.* Thousand Oaks, CA: Corwin.

Cherry, D., & Spiegel, J. (2006). *Leadership, myth, & metaphor: Finding common ground to guide effective school change.* Thousand Oaks, CA: Corwin.

Collier, C. (2010). *Seven steps to separating difference from disability.* Thousand Oaks, CA: Corwin.

Cooper, J. E., He, Y., & Levin, B. B. (2011). *Developing critical cultural competence: A guide for 21st century educators.* Thousand Oaks, CA: Corwin.

Creighton, T. B. (2007). *Schools and data: The educator's guide for using data to improve decision making* (2nd ed.). Thousand Oaks, CA: Corwin.

Danielson, C., & McCrea, T. L. (2000). *Teacher evaluation to enhance professional practice.* Princeton, NJ: Educational Testing Service.

Daresh, J. (2001). *Leaders helping leaders: A practical guide to administrative mentoring* (2nd ed.). Thousand Oaks, CA: Corwin.

Daresh, J. C. (2002). *Teachers mentoring teachers: A practical approach to helping new and experienced staff.* Thousand Oaks, CA: Corwin.

Deli'Olio, J., & Donk, T. (2007). *Models of teaching: Connecting student learning with standards.* Thousand Oaks, CA: Sage.

Denmark, V. M., & Podsen, I. J. (2000). *Coaching and mentoring first-year and student teachers.* Larchmont, NY: Eye on Education.

Downey, C. J., Steffy, B. E., Poston, W. K., Jr., & English, F. W. (2009). *Advancing the three-minute walk-through: Mastering reflective practice.* Thousand Oaks, CA: Corwin.

Earl, L. M., & Katz, S. (2006). *Leading schools in a data-rich world: Harnessing data for school improvement.* Thousand Oaks, CA: Corwin.

English, F. W. (2000). *Deciding what to teach and test: Developing, aligning, and auditing the curriculum.* Thousand Oaks, CA: Corwin.

Erickson, L. H. (2002). *Concept-based curriculum and instruction: Teaching beyond the facts.* Thousand Oaks, CA: Corwin.

Fichtman Dana, N., & Yendol-Hoppey, D. (2008). *The reflective educator's guide to professional development: Coaching inquiry-oriented learning communities.* Thousand Oaks, CA: Corwin.

Ford, B. A., & Obiakor, F. E. (2002). *Creating successful learning environments for African American learners with exceptionalities.* Thousand Oaks, CA: Corwin.

Glanz, J. (2003). *Action research: An educational guide to school improvement.* Norwood, MA: Christopher Gordon.

Glatthorn, A. A. (2001). *The principal as curriculum leader* (2nd ed.). Thousand Oaks, CA: Corwin.

Glatthorn, A. A., Boshcee, F., & Bruce, W. M. (2006). *Curriculum leadership: Development and implementation.* Thousand Oaks, CA: Sage.

Grady, M. L., & Brock, B. L. (2001). *From first-year to first-rate: Principals guiding beginning teachers.* Thousand Oaks, CA: Corwin.

Gregory, G. H., & Chapman, C. (2007). *Differentiated instructional strategies: One size doesn't fit all.* Thousand Oaks, CA: Corwin.

Guskey, T. R. (2000). *Evaluating professional development.* Thousand Oaks, CA: Corwin.

Hadaway, N., Vardell, S. M., & Young, T. (2001). *Literature-based instruction with English language learners.* Boston, MA: Allyn & Bacon.

Holt, L. C., & Kysika, M. (2006). *Instructional patterns: Strategies for maximizing student learning.* Thousand Oaks, CA: Sage.

Howard, T., Dresser, S. G., & Dunklee, D. R. (2009). *Poverty is not a learning disability: Equalizing opportunities for low SES students.* Thousand Oaks, CA: Corwin.

Hoyle, J. H., English, F., & Steffy, B. (1998). *Skills for successful 21st century school leaders.* Arlington, VA: American Association of School Administrators.

Irby, B. J., & Brown, G. (2000). *The career advancement portfolio.* Thousand Oaks, CA: Corwin.

Jarvis, P. (2007). *Lifelong learning and the learning society: Requirements and provision.* Florence, KY: Routledge.

Johnson, R. S. (2002). *Using data to close the achievement gap: How to measure equity in our schools.* Thousand Oaks, CA: Corwin.

Johnson, R. S., Mims-Cox, J. S., & Doyle-Nichols, A. (2006). *Developing portfolios in education: A guide to reflection, inquiry, and assessment.* Thousand Oaks, CA: Sage.

Joyner, E. T., Ben-Avie, M., & Comer, J. P. (2004). *Transforming school leadership and management to support student learning and development: The field guide to Comer schools in action.* Thousand Oaks, CA: Corwin.

Joyner, E. T., Comer, J. P., & Ben-Avie, M. (2004). *Comer schools in action: The 3-volume field guide.* Thousand Oaks, CA: Corwin.

Kee, K., Anderson, K., Dearing, V., Harris, E., & Shuster, F. (2010). *Results coaching: The new essential for school leaders.* Thousand Oaks, CA: Corwin.

Kennedy, E. (2003). *Raising test scores for all students: An administrator's guide to improving standardized test performance.* Thousand Oaks, CA: Corwin.

Kimmelman, P. L. (2006). *Implementing NCLB: Creating a knowledge framework to support school improvement.* Thousand Oaks, CA: Corwin.

Knight, J. (2007). *Instructional coaching: A partnership approach to improving instruction.* Thousand Oaks, CA: Corwin.

Kozol, J. (1992). *Savage inequalities: Children in America's schools.* New York, NY: Harper.

Kozol, J. (2000). *Ordinary resurrections: Children in the years of hope.* New York, NY: Crown.

Love, N. (2009). *Using data to improve learning for all: A collaborative inquiry approach.* Thousand Oaks, CA: Corwin.

Love, N., Stiles, K. E., Mundry, S., & DiRanna, K. (2008). *The data coach's guide to improving learning for all students: Unleashing the power of collaborative inquiry.* Thousand Oaks, CA: Corwin.

Maanum, J. L. (2009). *The general educator's guide to special education* (3rd ed.). Thousand Oaks, CA: Corwin.

Madigan, J. B., & Schroth-Cavataio, G. (2011). *Mentorship of special educators.* Thousand Oaks, CA: Corwin.

Mandinach, E. B., & Jackson, S. S. (2012). *Transforming teaching and learning through data-driven decision making: Classroom insights from educational psychology.* Thousand Oaks, CA: Corwin.

Martin, L. C. (2009). *Strategies for teaching students with learning disabilities.* Thousand Oaks, CA: Corwin.

McCabe, N., Cunningham, L. L., Harvey, J., & Koff, R. H. (2005). *The superintendent's fieldbook: A guide for leaders of learning.* Thousand Oaks, CA: Corwin.

McLaughlin, M. J. (2008). *What every principal needs to know about special education* (2nd ed.). Thousand Oaks, CA: Corwin.

McTighe, J., & Arter, J. (2001). *Scoring rubrics in the classroom: Using performance criteria for assessing and improving student performance.* Thousand Oaks, CA: Corwin.

Metzger, C. (2006). *Balancing leadership and personal growth: The school administrator's guide.* Thousand Oaks, CA: Corwin.

Monahan, T. (2005). *Globalization, technological change, and public education.* New York, NY: Routledge.

Montgomery, K., & Wiley, D. (2004). *Creating E-portfolios using PowerPoint: A guide for educators.* Thousand Oaks, CA: Sage.

Moore, K. (2005). *Effective instructional strategies: From theory to practice.* Thousand Oaks, CA: Sage.

Morel, N. J., & Cushman, C. S. (2012). *How to build an instructional coaching program for maximum capacity.* Thousand Oaks, CA: Corwin.

Moxley, D. E., & Taylor, R. T. (2006). *Literacy coaching: A handbook for school leaders.* Thousand Oaks, CA: Corwin.

Murawski, W. W., & Spencer, S. (2011). *Collaborate, communicate, and differentiate!* Thousand Oaks, CA: Corwin.

Nicholls, G. (2005). *The challenge to scholarship: Rethinking learning, teaching and research.* New York, NY: Routledge Falmer.

Nicoll, K. (2006). *Flexibility and lifelong learning: Policy, discourse and politics.* New York, NY: Routledge.

Nielsen, L. B. (2002). *Brief reference of student disabilities.* Thousand Oaks, CA: Corwin.

Osborne, A. G., & Russo, C. J. (2009). *Discipline in special education.* Thousand Oaks, CA: Corwin.

Payne, R. K. (2005). *A framework for understanding poverty.* Baytown, TX: RFT.

Peterson, K. D. (2002). *Effective teacher hiring: A guide to getting the best.* Alexandria, VA: Association for Supervision & Curriculum Development.

Podsen, I. J. (2002). *Teacher retention: What is your weakest link?* Larchmont, NY: Eye on Education.

Popham, W. J. (2010). *Everything school leaders need to know about assessment.* Thousand Oaks, CA: Corwin.

Reiss, K. (2006). *Leadership coaching for educators: Bringing out the best in school administrators.* Thousand Oaks, CA: Corwin.

Reksten, L. E. (2000). *Using technology to increase student learning.* Thousand Oaks, CA: Corwin.

Reksten, L. E. (2009). *Sustaining extraordinary student achievement.* Thousand Oaks, CA: Corwin.

Robinson, V., & Lai, M. K. (2006). *Practitioner research for educators: A guide to improving classrooms and schools.* Thousand Oaks, CA: Corwin.

Sagor, R. (2005). *The action research guidebook.* Thousand Oaks, CA: Corwin.

Schlechty, P. C. (2001). *Shaking up the school house.* San Francisco, CA: Jossey-Bass.

Schmuck, R. (2006). *Practical action research for change.* (2nd ed.). Thousand Oaks, CA: Corwin.

Sergiovanni, T. J. (2000). *The lifeworld of leadership: Creating culture, community, and personal meaning in our schools.* San Francisco, CA: Jossey-Bass.

Showers, B., & Joyce, B. (2002). *Student achievement through staff development* (3rd ed.). Alexandria, VA: Association for Supervision & Curriculum Development.

Singleton, G. E., & Linton, C. (2005). *Courageous conversations about race: A field guide for achieving equity in schools.* Thousand Oaks, CA: Corwin.

Solomon, P. G. (2002). *The assessment bridge: Positive ways to link tests to learning, standards, and curriculum improvement.* Thousand Oaks, CA: Corwin.

Sorenson, R. C., Goldsmith, L. M., Mendez, Z. Y., & Maxwell, K. T. (2011). *The principal's guide to curriculum leadership.* Thousand Oaks, CA: Corwin.

Strickland, C. A., & Glass, K. T. (2009). *Staff development guide for the parallel curriculum.* Thousand Oaks, CA: Corwin.

Sunderman, G. L. (2008). *Holding NCLB accountable: Achieving accountability, equity, & school reform.* Thousand Oaks, CA: Corwin.

Sunderman, G. L., Kim, J. S., & Orfield, G. (2005). *NCLB meets school realities: Lessons from the field.* Thousand Oaks, CA: Corwin.

Thompson, R., Kitchie, L., & Gagnon, R. (2011). *Constructing an online professional learning network for school unity and student achievement.* Thousand Oaks, CA: Corwin.

Thompson, S. J., Quenemoen, R. F., Thurlow, M. L., & Ysseldyke, J. E. (2001). *Alternate assessments for students with disabilities.* Thousand Oaks, CA: Corwin.

Tileston, D. W., & Darling, S. K. (2009). *Teaching students of poverty and diverse culture.* Thousand Oaks, CA: Corwin.

Tomlinson, C. A. (2001). *How to differentiate instruction in mixed-ability classrooms* (2nd ed.). Alexandria, VA: Association for Supervision & Curriculum Development.

Tomlinson, C. A., & Allan, S. D. (2000). *Leadership for differentiating schools and classrooms.* Alexandria, VA: Association for Supervision & Curriculum Development.

Townsend, R. S., Johnston, G. L., Gross, G. E., Lynch, R., Garcy, L., Roberts, B., et al. (2007). *Effective superintendent-school board practices: Strategies for developing and maintaining good relationships with your board.* Thousand Oaks, CA: Corwin.

Walker, E., Sather, S. E., Norte, E., Katz, A., & Henze, R. C. (2002). *Leading for diversity: How school leaders promote interethnic relations.* Thousand Oaks, CA: Corwin.

Whitehead, B. M., Jensen, D. F. N., & Boschee, F. (2002). *Planning for technology: A guide for school administrators, technology coordinators, and curriculum leaders.* Thousand Oaks, CA: Corwin.

Williams, R. B. (2008). *Twelve roles of facilitators for school change* (2nd ed.). Thousand Oaks, CA: Corwin.

Wilmore, E. L. (2004). *Principal induction: A standards-based model for administrator development.* Thousand Oaks, CA: Corwin.

Wilmore, E. L. (2007). *Teacher leadership: Improving teaching and learning from inside the classroom.* Thousand Oaks, CA: Corwin.

Wolfe, P. (2001). *Brain matters: Translating research into classroom practice.* Alexandria, VA: Association for Supervision & Curriculum Development.

Woodward, J., & Cuban, L. (Eds.). (2001). *Technology, curriculum, and professional development: Adapting schools to meet the needs of students with disabilities.* Thousand Oaks, CA: Corwin.

Worthen, B., Sanders, J., & Fitzpatrick, J. (2010). *Program evaluation, alternative approaches and practical guidelines.* (4th ed.). New York, NY: Addison-Wesley.

Ybarra, S., Hollingsworth, J., & Ardovino, J. (2000). *Multiple measures: Accurate ways to assess student achievement.* Thousand Oaks, CA: Corwin.

Yendol-Hoppey, D., & Dane, N. F. (2010). *Powerful professional development.* Thousand Oaks, CA: Corwin.

DOMAIN III: ADMINISTRATIVE LEADERSHIP

Anderson, J. W. (2001). *The answers to questions that teachers most frequently ask.* Thousand Oaks, CA: Corwin.

Bennis, W. (1997). *Managing people is like herding cats.* Provo, UT: Executive Excellence.

Bjork, L. G., & Kowalski, T. J. (2005). *The contemporary superintendent: Preparation, practice, and development.* Thousand Oaks, CA: Corwin.

Brewer, E. W., Achilles, C. M., Fuhriman, J. R., & Hollingsworth, C. (2001). *Finding funding: Grant writing from start to finish, including project management and Internet use.* Thousand Oaks, CA: Corwin.

Brunner, J. M., & Lewis, D. K. (2009). *Safe & secure schools: 27 strategies for prevention and intervention.* Thousand Oaks, CA: Corwin.

Burrup, P. E., Brimpley, V., Jr., & Garfield, R. R. (2012). *Financing education in a climate of change* (11th ed.). Boston, MA: Allyn & Bacon.

Bush, T., & Middlewood, D. (2005). *Leading and managing people in education.* Thousand Oaks, CA: Sage.

Cambron-McCabe, N. (2005). *The superintendent's fieldbook.* Thousand Oaks, CA: Corwin.

Coleman, M., & Anderson, L. (2000). *Managing finance and resources in education.* Thousand Oaks, CA: Corwin.

Collinson, V., & Cook, T. F. (2006*). Organizational learning: Improving learning, teaching, and leading in school systems.* Thousand Oaks, CA: Sage.

Covey, S. R. (1990). *The 7 habits of highly effective people.* New York, NY: Simon & Schuster.

DiGiulio, R. C. (2001). *Educate, medicate, or litigate? What teachers, parents, and administrators must do about student behavior.* Thousand Oaks, CA: Corwin.

Dunklee, D. R., & Shoop, R. J. (2006). *The principal's quick-reference guide to school law: Reducing liability, litigation, and other potential legal tangles.* Thousand Oaks, CA: Corwin.

Eller, J., & Carlson, H. C. (2009). *So now you're the superintendent!* Thousand Oaks, CA: Corwin.

Fullan, M. (2005). *Leadership sustainability: System thinkers in action.* Thousand Oaks, CA: Corwin.

Hoyle, J. R., Bjork, L. G., Collier, V., & Glass, T. (2005). *The superintendent as CEO: Standards-based performance.* Thousand Oaks, CA: Corwin.

Imber, M., & Van Geel, T. (2000). *Education law* (2nd ed.). Mahwah, NJ: Lawrence Erlbaum Associates.

Knowles, C. (2002). *The first time grant writer's guide to success.* Thousand Oaks, CA: Corwin.

Levenson, S. (2006). *Big-time fundraising for today's schools.* Thousand Oaks, CA: Corwin.

Lunenburg, F. C., & Ornstein, A. C. (2000). *Educational administration: Concepts and practices* (3rd ed.). Belmont, CA: Wadsworth/Thomas Learning.

Marazza, L. L. (2003). *The five essentials of organizational excellence: Maximizing school wide student achievement and performance.* Thousand Oaks, CA: Corwin.

McNeal, B., & Oxholm, T. (2009). *A school district's journey to excellence: Lessons from business and education.* Thousand Oaks, CA: Corwin.

Meyer, L. H., & Evans, I. M. (2012). *The school leader's guide to restorative school discipline.* Thousand Oaks, CA: Corwin.

Miles, K. H., & Frank, S. (2008). *The strategic school: Making the most of people, time, and money.* Thousand Oaks, CA: Corwin.

Odden, A. (2012). *Improving student learning when budgets are tight.* Thousand Oaks, CA: Corwin.

Odden, A., & Archibald, S. (2001). *Reallocating resources: How to boost student achievement without asking for more.* Thousand Oaks, CA: Corwin.

Olsen, K. D. (2010). *What brain research can teach about cutting school budgets.* Thousand Oaks, CA: Corwin.

Osborne, A. G., Jr., & Russo, C. J. (2011). *The legal rights and responsibilities of teachers: Issues of employment and instruction.* Thousand Oaks, CA: Corwin.

Parsons, B. A. (2001). *Evaluative inquiry: Using evaluation to promote student success.* Thousand Oaks, CA: Corwin.

Peterson, S. (2001). *The grant writer's Internet companion: A resource for educators and others seeking grants and funding.* Thousand Oaks, CA: Corwin.

Poston, W. K., Jr. (2010). *School budgeting for hard times: Confronting cutbacks and critics.* Thousand Oaks, CA: Corwin.

Ramsey, R. D. (2001). *Fiscal fitness for school administrators: How to stretch resources and do even more with less.* Thousand Oaks, CA: Corwin.

Sanders, J. R. (2000). *Evaluating school programs* (2nd ed.). Thousand Oaks, CA: Corwin.

Schimmel, D., Eckes, S., & Militello, M. (2010). *Principals teaching the law: 10 legal lessons your teachers must know.* Thousand Oaks, CA: Corwin.

Schroth, G., Berkeley, T. R., & Fishbaugh, M. S. (2003). *Ensuring safe school environments.* Mahwah, NJ: Lawrence Erlbaum Associates.

Sergiovanni, T. J. (2000). *The lifeworld of leadership.* San Francisco, CA: Jossey-Bass.

Shoop, R. J., & Dunklee, D. R. (2006). *Anatomy of a lawsuit: What every education leader should know about legal actions.* Thousand Oaks, CA: Corwin.

Sorenson, R. D., & Goldsmith, L. M. (2012). *The principal's guide to school budgeting.* Thousand Oaks, CA: Corwin.

Thomson, S. (Ed.). (1993). *Principals of our changing schools: Knowledge and skill base.* Alexandria, VA: National Policy Board for Educational Administration.

Trolley, B. C., & Hanel, C. (2009). *Cyber kids, cyber bullying, cyber balance.* Thousand Oaks, CA: Corwin.

Winslade, J., & Williams, M. (2011). *Safe and peaceful schools: Addressing conflict and eliminating violence.* Thousand Oaks, CA: Corwin.

Index

CORWIN

A SAGE Company

The Corwin logo—a raven striding across an open book—represents the union of courage and learning. Corwin is committed to improving education for all learners by publishing books and other professional development resources for those serving the field of PreK–12 education. By providing practical, hands-on materials, Corwin continues to carry out the promise of its motto: **"Helping Educators Do Their Work Better."**